C000265369

NATURAL DYES FOR
SPINNERS
& WEAVERS

Hetty Wickens

NATURAL DYES FOR SPINNERS & WEAVERS

B T Batsford Limited, London

© Hetty Wickens 1983
First published 1983

All rights reserved. No part of this publication
may be reproduced, in any form or by any means,
without permission from the Publisher

ISBN 0 7134 2021 9

Typeset by D.P. Press Ltd
and printed in Great Britain by
The Anchor Press Ltd
Tiptree, Essex
for the publishers
B. T. Batsford Ltd.
4 Fitzhardinge Street
London W1H 0AH

Contents

Acknowledgment

I would like to thank all those people who have helped me to collect the information for this book. My practical experience has been gained by working with many well-known dyers and with enthusiastic members of Guilds of Weavers, Spinners and Dyers.

The majority of black and white photographs were taken by my nephew Christopher Pedley and the flower photographs by William Robertson who had a dye garden in Scotland. Photographs of sheep were supplied by the British Wool Marketing Board.

My requests for information have been willingly and promptly answered by Elizabeth Scholtz, Director, Brooklyn Botanic Garden, USA; Ralph Broadhurst, Curator of the Colour Museum, Bradford; Darrel Bailey from Sydney, Australia; Joan Rippengal from Eastbourne; Norman T. Wills from Spalding and Heather Tredgett from Pontefract.

Finally, I would like to thank Meta Joyce for typing the manuscript and Stuart Robinson for reading and checking it.

The extract from S. Robertson's *Dyes from Plants* (1973) is reprinted by permission of Van Nostrand Reinhold Company.

Introduction

This book is a guide to the use of natural dye-stuffs. Many people wonder why it is worthwhile going to all the trouble of collecting flowers, leaves, berries and roots when it would be much easier to buy a packet of dye powder. It would be easier, in some cases cheaper and certainly less time-consuming. As a commercial proposition natural dyeing would be financially uneconomic, but it can become an absorbing hobby which enriches one's life in many directions. It is rightly said that synthetic dyes can do anything a natural dye can and that the colours can be matched exactly. But how can an exact colour match be made if there is no naturally dyed colour to compare it with in the first place?

Natural dyeing is challenging: we have lost many of the old dyer's skills — can we re-discover them? Apart from mordanting, dyeing can be as simple as boiling fruit or vegetables. Everything that is needed to make a start is available in most kitchens. Waste materials such as onion skins, carrot-tops, tea and coffee bags and flower heads can be used.

It is possible to gain great satisfaction from producing one's own colours. This practical work encourages one to look at colours differently, to analyse colour schemes, to consider colour theories. Knowledge is extended, since it is helpful to the dyer to find out more about chemistry, botany, history, geography and mathematics.

1
Preparation

Dyeing with natural dyestuffs can be as casual or as serious as the individual likes to make it. Colours are obtained easily, merely by boiling plants, berries, leaves, bark or flower heads. It is as simple as cooking fruit or vegetables. When permanent colours are required, most dyes need a mordant to fix the colour. This is the time when great care and accuracy are needed; successful mordanting leads to successful dyeing, and it is therefore of the utmost importance.

Minimum equipment

When starting to dye very little equipment is necessary; all the requirements will probably be found in the kitchen.

Minimum requirements are:

Water

Dye-bath — which could be a saucepan or pot

Stirring rods

Spoons

Material to dye

Dyestuff

A method of heating

Equipment found in a kitchen

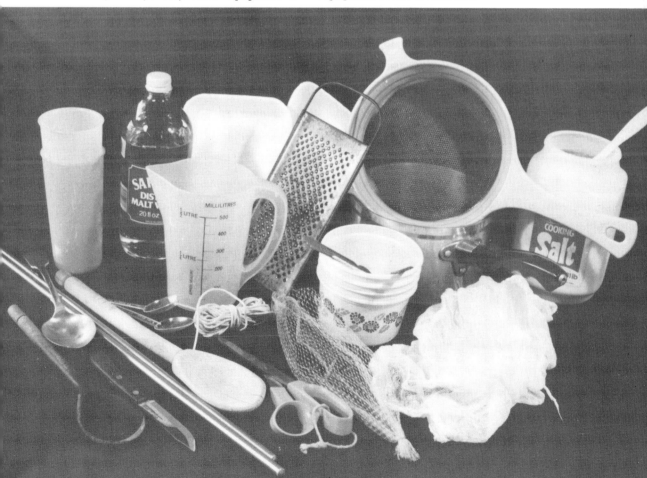

Dyestuffs

Natural dyestuffs are to be found all around, in the garden, the fields, hedgerows and woods. Waste materials also provide useful sources, including tea and coffee bags, carrot-tops, onion skins, leaves from vegetables and discarded flowers from the garden.

Always be ready to experiment and build up a collection of dyestuffs. There is plenty of scope for individual discoveries. We all have our own ways of working and our interpretations of recipes will probably be quite different from other people's. Dyers are said to be very secretive and that is why today we find it almost impossible to reproduce some of the bright and unusual colours of the early dyers. Recipes were handed down from father to son; individuals must have added a pinch of this or that and they had the skill to judge the right moment to simmer, cool and rinse.

Flowers

Flower heads give the brightest colours when they are fresh and in full bloom — when they are fading their colours are less bright. If they are dirty, wash them and then soak them in cold water for a few hours or overnight. Less time will be required for heating if the flower heads are soaked and this will be an advantage when dyeing yellow or red colours. Heat destroys anthocyanins, the pigments which produce many colours in flowers and plants. (Incidentally, anthocyanins are used in colouring food.) A low simmer of about 80°C is recommended during dyeing. Examine the colour every 20 minutes or so and be ready to remove the yarn when the colour is right. Remember that the colour will look darker when it is wet. Flowers can be tied in a muslin bag or nylon net to prevent them getting mixed up in the wool, or the liquid can be strained.

Berries

On the whole, the strongest colours will be obtained from berries if they are picked when ripe. Make sure they are clean so that there is no dirt to dull the colour. If the berries are hard, crush them with a hammer and soak for several hours — it takes longer to extract the colour from solid sources. Colour runs freely from blackberries, elderberries and bilberries. The liquid can be strained and kept in the refrigerator for future use or the berries can be frozen until required. It is very helpful to have a supply of berries in the freezer to use throughout the year. Violetta Thurstan, a well-known English dyer, used to say 'Bilberries make a good colour — if you can bear to go without them in a pie'. Berries can also be dried on a wire-mesh tray until they shrivel and then stored in a muslin or net bag. Berries must not be stored in a damp state for they will ferment, go rotten and smell horrible.

Barks

Hard substances such as barks, roots, cones and hulls will produce colours, but it may take a little longer to extract the dye. Tree bark can be obtained from recently felled trees, from broken branches or from twigs which have been pruned. After pruning, collect twigs that are at least two years old, as these have more dye content than younger shoots. Do not peel bark from the entire circumference of a living tree, for this will kill it. Colours from bark are influenced by the tannin content so they are usually yellow to apricot, tan and brown. Black is obtained from some trees. Spring and autumn are the best times for collecting wood and twigs, when the sap is most active.

Wash the bark before using it, cut it up into small pieces and soak overnight. Simmering for at least two hours is necessary in order to extract the colour. The liquid can be sieved and stored in opaque jars. On the other hand, wood can be dried completely, labelled and put away for future use.

Roots

Roots are usually strongest in autumn when the plant is preparing to store its winter food. Dandelion and dock roots can be completely uprooted, but take care if using roots from a tree or shrub. Dig out only parts of the root to avoid injury to the plant. Dandelion roots have always been a great disappointment to me. Scottish dyers are said to have obtained magenta from dandelion roots, but I have only obtained a dirty yellow. (My dandelions grew in Sussex.)

Cones and hulls

Pick cones when they are open so that the sap does not cling to the wool. Hulls from walnuts give the strongest colour when they are green but they can be used when they have turned black.

Leaves

Leaves should be gathered when they are mature. Supple green leaves such as nettle and bracken should be collected and used at once in order to obtain the clearest yellowish green. Some leaves are tougher and need breaking before being boiled.

Woad leaves should be broken into small pieces before being boiled; weld leaves can be used at once or after harvesting. Strip leaves from twigs so that there is no danger of tannin making the colour dull.

Choice of room

The kitchen is a good place to work in, provided one can make satisfactory arrangements with other occupants of the house. In a kitchen one usually has a stove, sink, hot and cold water, scales, a table, spoons, pans, buckets, measuring jugs, sieves, spin drier, paper towels and a waste bin. Take care if dangerous chemicals are being used; however, if you are starting with alum as a mordant there should be no problem. Aluminium potassium sulphate (alum) is a safe and popular mordant to use.

If you are able to set aside a room or part of a room especially for dyeing consider these points:

The height of working benches and heating apparatus

A large gas ring near the floor will enable one to avoid lifting heavy dye-baths from a height. It will allow the dyer to look into the bath easily and assess what is happening to the liquor and yarn. Consider the height of the working bench in relation to your own height. If possible choose a surface which is easy to clean, such as formica.

Storage space

Have plenty of shelves around the room and con-veniently placed cupboards. Large hooks will be useful for hanging bags of dyestuff or bundles of plants. I like to have a cupboard which locks for storage of chemicals and dyestuffs so that they can be kept in a safe place, and a shelf or book-case near the workbench where small quantities of chemicals can be kept. Near the sink I have a collection of useful odds and ends. These include a selection of sticks, rods, spoons, cream pots, margarine cartons, coffee jars with screw top lids, paper towels, raffia, tape and oddments of cotton yarn. The cartons are very useful because they will stand inside each other and take up little space.

Floor covering

Have something which can be cleaned easily. Modern plastic tiles are satisfactory but make sure they are kept dry.

Sinks

If you are free to choose the position of the sink allow plenty of room around it; often sinks are pushed into a corner. A stainless steel double sink with a double-drainer is desirable, but if space is limited it is possible to buy a double sink with a fixed drainer on one side and a detachable one which can be moved from side to side or placed on top of one sink.

Mixer taps are an advantage, especially when preparing rinsing water. While thinking of water-supply, consider installing a water softener if your water is hard.

Ventilation

The room should be light and well-ventilated. A large amount of steam is often produced during dyeing.

Lighting

If colour is critical, consider the type of lighting.

Position of the room

Ideally the room should be situated near the garden so that the drying ground is easily accessible.

Power points

If using electricity have plenty of power points

arranged in convenient positions. Avoid the need for trailing flexes.

Useful equipment

Dye vessels

These include dye-baths, pots, saucepans or vessels. I usually describe the vessel as a dye-bath whatever its shape. A dye-bath can be made of different materials, but these materials can affect the resulting colours. Stainless steel is an excellent but expensive choice. It can easily be kept clean, so the expense is usually worth it. Cleanliness is a very important aspect of dyeing. Traces of unwanted colour can be disastrous, or on the other hand they may be just what was wanted. Unchipped enamel makes a satisfactory dye-bath. Pans made of aluminium, copper or iron can affect the resulting colours. Often these pans are chosen on purpose in order to obtain a brighter or duller colour. If an unusual colour appears, try to discover the reason so that it can be repeated if necessary. There must be many secrets belonging to dyers of ancient days which we may rediscover if we keep our eyes open and record experiments and results methodically.

Stirring rods

These form a valuable part of the equipment. Stainless steel rods are the first choice, followed by strong glass rods or smooth wooden ones. Never use rough wood because the slightest trace of roughness clings to woollen fibres. Old warp sticks, if smooth, are suitable for stirring but are not usually strong enough for lifting skeins out of boiling liquid. Wooden rods get stained so they must be kept clean. Large wooden spoons are useful. The rods used for lifting out skeins from the dye-bath need to be strong and long so that they will not break when lifting heavy skeins from hot liquor. The yarn could fall back into the dye causing splashes.

Scales

When weighing mordants scales which will weigh grams are virtually essential, as the amounts to be weighed are very small. Those used for weighing letters or food for some specialized diets will be satisfactory. Never place the chemicals straight into the pan, but weigh onto a piece of paper, remembering to adjust the scales to take its weight into account. Ordinary household scales can be used for weighing dyestuffs.

Thermometer

A long thermometer which can be used to check the temperature at the bottom of the dye-bath as well as the top is required. With experience it will be fairly easy to judge the temperature.

Measuring jugs and spoons

Pyrex or strong plastic measuring jugs and spoons of various sizes should be kept handy. Chemists supply 5 ml (.17 fl oz) spoons with medicine.

Indicator paper

This paper is necessary when testing the acidity or alkalinity of the water (see page 26).

Other useful equipment

All kinds of oddments are useful: plastic spoons, stainless steel knife for chopping hard dyestuffs, grater, sieve, colander, net bags from the greengrocer, rubber gloves or thin plastic ones which are available in packets, labels and waterproof pens. A wringer is helpful if large quantities of yarn are being dyed but with an efficient spin drier this is not so necessary. Tumbler driers are not to be recommended because wool could get felted. Paper towels, old towels and scraps of rag all serve a useful purpose, as do odd lengths of tape, string, raffia and undyed cotton. Newspapers are useful for covering surfaces but it is also a good idea to make them into a pad of convenient size. For example, small newspapers or telephone directories can be torn up into separate sheets and kept in the form of a pad. If chemicals should be spilt during measuring it is easier to throw away a small sheet from the pad than a large piece of paper which had been covering the table.

Useful chemicals

Aluminium potassium sulphate (alum)

Potassium dichromate (chrome)

Ferrous sulphate (iron)

Stannous chloride (tin)

Potassium hydrogen tartrate (cream of tartar)

Sodium sulphate (Glauber's Salts)

Sodium carbonate (washing soda)

Sodium chloride (common salt)

Acetic acid (vinegar is a weak solution of acetic acid)

Calcium oxide (lime)

Sodium hydroxide (caustic soda)

Sodium dithionite (formerly called sodium hydro-sulphite)

Ammonium hydroxide (household ammonia). CAUTION : Take care when using

Always keep the jars accurately labelled. They should have well-fitting lids and should be kept in a safe place — especially if the kitchen is your dye house.

Weights and measures

Although measurements have been given in the metric and imperial systems dyers who are not familiar with the metric system may find these equivalents helpful:

1 ounce (oz)　　= 28.349 grams (g)
1 pound (lb)　　= .453 kilograms (kg) 453g
2.2 pounds (lb) = 1 kilogram (kg)

These approximate equivalents are useful if working with old recipes given in imperial measurements:

approximate equivalents
1 oz　　= 30 g
½ lb　　= 250 g
1 lb　　= .5 kg
2 lb　　= 1 kg
1 gallon = 4.5 litres

NB When weighing chemicals to be used as mordants great accuracy is absolutely essential. Approximate or generous weights are satisfactory for most plants.

Temperatures

The terms cold, warm, hand heat, simmering and boiling are used in recipes. The following temperatures expressed in centigrade give an indication of the numbers to be registered on the thermometer:

cold $0°-5°C$

warm approximately $20°C$

hand-heat $39°-49°C$ Water should feel hot to the hand (just over $36°C$ is body temperature).

simmering $82°-93°C$ There is a slight movement on the water. This will vary according to whether it is a high simmer or a low simmer

boiling $100°C$

Notebooks and records

One should always get into the habit of keeping records of dye recipes and their results. As well as a written record, samples should also be mounted and labelled. Methods should be evolved which enable you to identify samples quickly and accurately. As samples may not be mounted until a later date do not remove the identification marks until permanent labels are made. I have always used the same method for identifying mordants, so there is never any doubt concerning the mordant used. Any thread with one overhand knot tells me that alum was used.

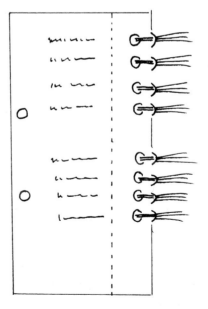

The card could be folded back on the dotted line to protect the samples

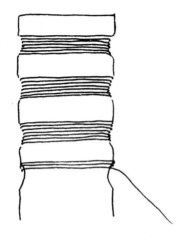

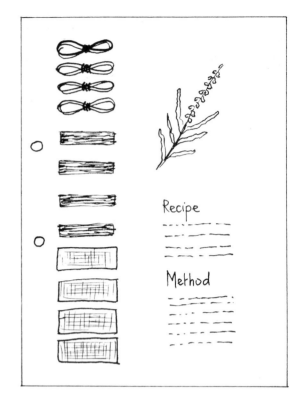

Above Winding threads round a stiff card

Right Mounting samples of spun yarn, fleece and woven cloth. These can be placed in a plastic envelope and fixed in a loose-leaf notebook

---

A typical page from a note-book

Blackthorn or Sloe (Prunus spinosa)

Date and time of gathering material 28 Sept 1981. 3 pm. Sunny day.

Place Hedgerow in Sussex village. Clay soil.

State of material 250 g (8 oz) ripe black berries (fairly hard).

Preparation of material Hammered, boiled in soft water one hour. Fruit strained. Liquid turned red.

Fibre to be dyed Four skeins of wool (30 g – 1 oz each).

Mordanting Each skein mordanted in one of the following: alum, chrome, iron or tin.

Dyeing The four skeins were simmered in dye-bath for 45 minutes.

Rinsing Half of each skein was given an acid rinse, the other half an alkaline rinse.

Colours obtained:

	Acid rinse	*Alkaline rinse*	*Observations*
Alum	Deep rose pink	Bluish red	The colour ran freely from the fruit. Alum mordant
Chrome	Brownish pink	No change	gave the clearest colour. When rinsed in a strong
Iron	Dull purple	No change	detergent the wool turned grey. After three weeks
Tin	Purple	No change	in a sunny window the colour was less bright.

Opposite Yarns prepared for testing in sunlight

14

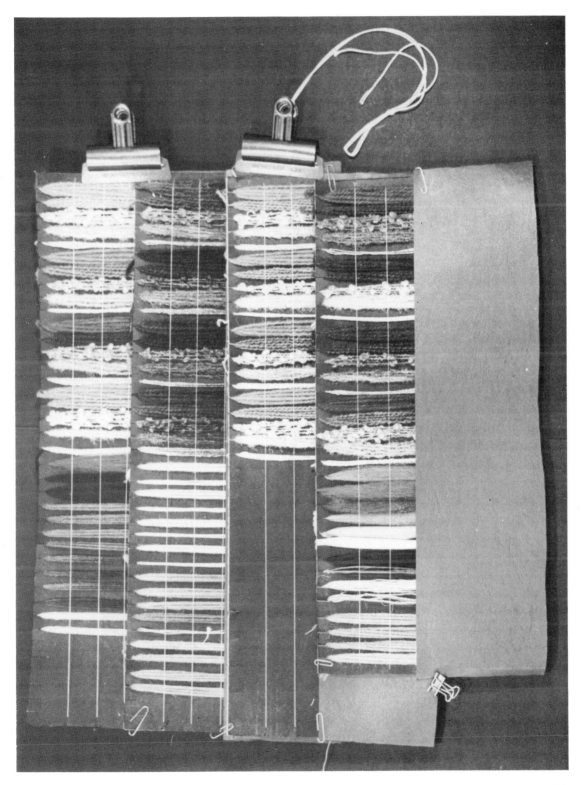

2
Selection and Preparation of Fibres

Wool

Wool is usually the first choice of fibre for dyeing. It is one of the easiest fibres to dye provided it is handled carefully. It is not enough just to say 'wool' — a discriminating dyer who is dyeing fleece will want to choose the quality of wool, and perhaps the part of the fleece from which it came.

There are many breeds of sheep and they provide a variety of fleeces. The wool can be dense, spongy, lustrous, coarse, fine, hairy, discoloured, grey, fawn or kempy.

The sheep can be divided into three groups according to the length of their wool:

1 *Short-wool breeds*. Down breeds come into this group. They include Southdown, Suffolk Down and Oxford Down. The wool from this group is short and soft with a tendency to felt.

Southdown sheep

2 *Medium-length.* Mountain breeds of sheep come into this category, including Welsh, Cheviot and Scottish Blackface. The wool is of medium-length, strong and sometimes harsh. Kemp is often found in these fleeces. Kemp is a dead, white hair which does not usually take the dye because it has a wide medulla. In some Welsh fleeces kemp can show up as red hairs. These hairs which do not dye like the rest of the wool can be used to add interest, but remove them if they are likely to spoil the desired effect.

3 *Long-wool breeds.* These include Lincoln, Leicester and Romney Marsh sheep. This wool is wavy, long and lustrous. It can be extremely useful when chosen carefully. If a small amount were mixed with a non-lustrous wool by mistake it could spoil a piece of work but if selected for its design value the result can be very attractive.

Natural-coloured fleeces
Natural-coloured fleeces are not looked upon with favour by dyers in the mills because a few coloured fibres could get into white wool by mistake and perhaps spoil the material. This probably would not show up until the scouring process was carried out. For the dyer at home, these natural-coloured fleeces are extremely useful. The light fawn and grey wool will dye well and add depth to a colour scheme. Dark brown wool from Jacob sheep and Black Welsh mountain sheep is unlikely to dye because it is too dark. However, in its natural state it can be used to blend with dyed wool.

Some fleeces contain grey wool and black hairs. Look out for these so that they do not appear by mistake.

Sorting fleece
When a fleece comes straight from the farmer it will consist of a variety of qualities. The dyer should be aware of the differences to be found on one fleece. Unroll the fleece, place it on the floor

Scottish Blackface sheep

Opposite above Lincoln Longwool sheep

Opposite below Jacob sheep

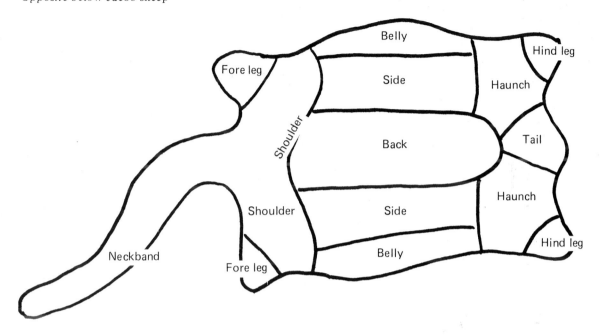

An opened-out fleece. Wool gets coarser towards the tail

with tips of fleece uppermost. Wool towards the tail will be the coarsest type while that over the back and shoulders will be of the best quality. Round the edge of the fleece there will be grey and dirty wool. Keep a number of cardboard boxes into which different grades of fleece can be placed.

Best quality wool will require a shorter time for mordanting than coarse wool. Every fleece will vary within each breed. If a very even colour is required great care must be taken at every stage to ensure that the same type of wool is being used. One of the advantages of dyeing wool in the fleece is that unevenness can disappear in the subsequent stage of carding.

Mohair, llama, alpaca and camel

If these are to be dyed, select the types of fibres required, remembering that soft fine fibres grow next to the body of the animal and coarse long ones on the outside.

Silk

Silk can be obtained in a variety of states — gummed, slivers or spun silk.

Cotton

Unless there is a special reason for wanting to dye cotton staple it is better to start with yarn. The yarn can come in the following states: unbleached, bleached or mercerized. It can be tightly, loosely or fancy spun.

Flax

Unspun flax is sold in bundles called stricks. It is a fawn colour so it will have to be bleached if a clear light colour is required. Spun linen can be bought in various stages of bleaching, from natural to brilliant white.

Sisal, hemp and jute give other opportunities for experimenting.

19

Man-made fibres

Rayon

Viscose rayon, being made from cellulose, will dye as for cotton. It can be obtained in the form of staple fibre or yarn.

Synthetic materials

These include nylon, terylene and dralon and can be obtained in staple form or yarn. Many handspinners prefer to ignore these materials but it is worth putting some into the dye-bath. They could add colour effects and in most cases they give added strength to the threads made from natural fibres.

Combed tops

Long fibres of wool and synthetic fibres can be dyed when they are in the form of combed tops.

Threads

Tightly twisted yarns are more difficult to dye

Various yarns suitable for dyeing

than loosely twisted ones because the dyestuff does not penetrate them so easily.

Woven cloth

Examine woven cloth to see what state it is in. 'In the grey' means that the cloth will be unwashed, just as it came from the loom. 'Finished' cloth may have gone through a special finishing process which could prevent the dye from penetrating the fibres. These finishes could include polishing, shrink-proofing, moth-proofing or fire-proofing.

Identification of fibres

These simple tests will help to identify yarns if there is a doubt concerning their content.

When burnt, wool smoulders and leaves a brown cinder. It smells of burnt hair. If boiled in a strong solution of caustic soda it disintegrates.

Vegetable fibres (cotton, linen, hemp, ramie) flame and burn quickly. They smell of burnt paper and leave a white ash. When boiled in a strong solution of caustic soda they turn brown.

Silk burns slowly and there is a smell of burnt hair. A little dark cinder is left at the end. Boiling in caustic soda solution dissolves silk.

Viscose rayon flames and burns quickly. It smells of burnt paper and swells when boiled in caustic soda solution.

Acetate rayon burns slowly without a smell. It melts into little balls at the end of the yarn. In a boiling solution of caustic soda it swells.

Nylon melts rather than burns, and a round hard fawn bead forms.

Stages in dyeing

We have considered dyeing fleece, combed tops, yarn and cloth, but dyeing can also take place on prepared warps and wefts (see pages 22, 83, 84).

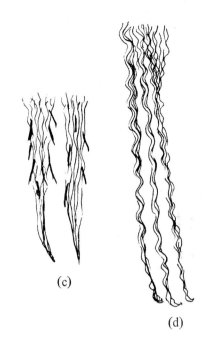

(c)

(d)

Stages in dyeing

Different types of fleece: (a) wavy (b) crimpy (c) with kemp (d) curly

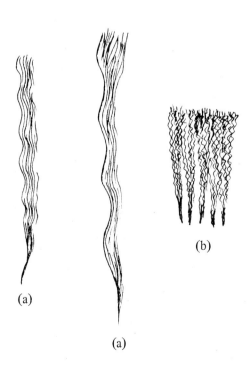

(a)

(b)

(a)

Combed tops

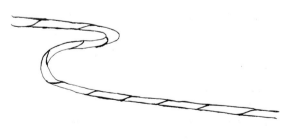

Roving which has been slightly twisted

21

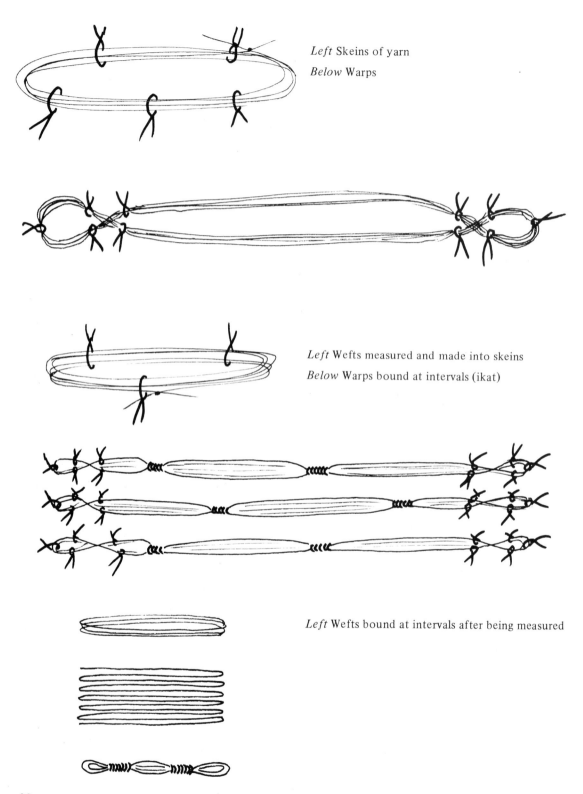

Left Skeins of yarn
Below Warps

Left Wefts measured and made into skeins
Below Warps bound at intervals (ikat)

Left Wefts bound at intervals after being measured

22

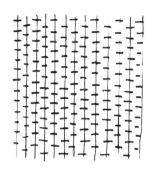

Woven cloth

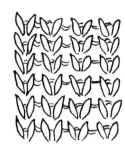

Knitted cloth

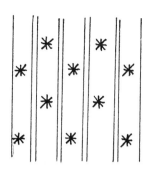

Printed cloth

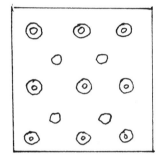

Tie-dyed cloth. Patterns made by tying the cloth before dyeing

Scouring or washing fleece

Before starting to wash the fleece look it over carefully. While doing so, pull the fibres apart, loosen them and remove vegetable matter such as bracken, leaves or thorns.

Wool must be thoroughly clean before being dyed so that there are no traces of natural grease, soluble salts (perspiration or suint), sand or dirt. Should soap or synthetic detergents be chosen? On the whole it is better to use the kind of detergent which you have proved to be satisfactory for your own laundry. Soap flakes help to leave the wool very soft, but they need to be carefully dissolved, and in the final rinsing care must be taken to remove all traces of soap. On the other hand, synthetic detergents dissolve quickly, especially those in liquid form.

The following are the most important points to remember:

1 Use plenty of soft water.

2 Soak the wool well.

3 Do not use water above a temperature of 55°C.

4 Never agitate wool violently or it may become felted or matted. Remember that wool is rubbed in alkaline solution to make it felt and shrink.

5 A little vinegar added to the rinsing water will help to neutralize an alkaline solution. Rinsing water should be lukewarm.

Procedure

Prepare a bath of hot soapy water (52–55°C) and allow the wool to stay in the bath overnight. This water will probably be dark grey or black if the wool was very dirty. One washing will not be enough to clean the wool so be prepared to soak, wash and rinse several times. Move the wool gently — there must be no violent agitating. After each wash, rinse the wool thoroughly in warm water. Gradually reduce the amount of soap used in each subsequent wash. Fleece can be placed in muslin or net before being lowered into the bath, which will make it easier to move it from one place to another. Always open out the wool so that every part becomes clean.

Once the wool is completely clean and free from grease and soap it can be dyed in its damp state. If it is not going to be used within the next two days it should be dried; this can be done by putting it in a spin drier first. Place the wool in a pillowcase or net bag, give it a spin and then hang in the open air to dry.

Skeins

Skeins of wool may be received in various states. Many hand-spinners prefer to spin their wool before scouring, so in this case thorough washing will be necessary to remove the grease.

If dyeing yarn in the form of skeins, there are several important points to note. It is extremely easy for skeins to get into a tangle, so take great care in their preparation. Most yarns used to be supplied in skein or hank form, but the majority now seem to come in balls or on cones and this means that one can get out of the habit of using skeins.

Making a skein

It may be necessary to make one's own skein first, so the dyer can decide on the length and weight of each one. On the whole it is better to make a number of smaller skeins rather than large, heavy ones. They are easier to handle and they give an opportunity to dye a larger variety of colours when making experiments. A skein of a given length is useful, especially to see if the yarn has shrunk during the various processes. For most experiments skeins weighing 30 g (1 oz) will be suitable.

The back of a chair, the end of a table, or warping posts make suitable equipment for winding skeins.

A tie-dyed skein partly untied

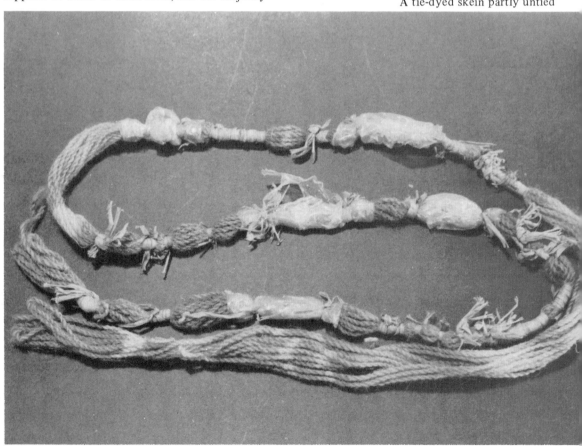

Sometimes I feel quite fanatical about the way skeins are tied, but this is because of the problems I have encountered with those people who are careless over the way they tie knots. I have tried leaving out some of the tedious stages of preparation but I have always regretted it. The smallest skeins seem to be able to get themselves into a terrible tangle if not treated properly and so much time is wasted in trying to wind up the yarn.

The following are the most important points to remember:

1 Tying the beginning and end of the yarn. Tie the two ends together; do not take them round the skein. Then tie a strong, uncoloured thread to them and take that round the skein. In a bought skein the two ends may be tied around it; if so untie and then retie them as in the diagram.

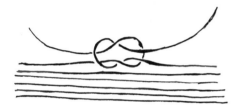

Tying the beginning and end of the skein

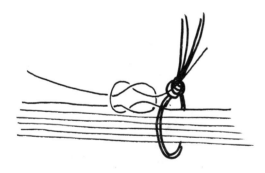

Tie a strong un-dyed thread to one end and take it right round the skein

2 The skein should be tied loosely in about four places so that it will not become tangled in all the processes which follow. Use uncoloured, fairly thick, strong thread for these ties so that they can be easily distinguished from the yarn at a later stage. Tie the ends together in a secure knot — the overhand knot is probably the safest. Leave

the ends about 5 cm (2 in.) long. If they are longer than this they can be troublesome, if shorter they do not give you the opportunity to retie if necessary. These ties are often useful for embroidery or for adding decorative effects in weaving. The ends of uncoloured warps provide useful yarn for tying. It is not wise to use coloured threads for ties unless a special effect is required, for the dye may not be fast.

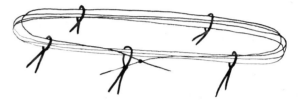

A skein tied in four places

Tied too tightly

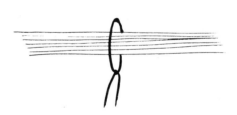

Tied too loosely

A safe way of tying, especially useful for slippery threads

25

Washing skeins

Having made a secure skein, check the state of the yarn. If it is very dirty and greasy treat as for greasy fleece, otherwise a gentle wash and rinse will be sufficient. Prepare a bath of warm soapy water and suspend the skeins on a tape so that they can be moved around gently.

After they have been washed and rinsed they will be evenly damp and in an ideal state for dyeing. If they are dried they will have to be evenly wetted-out before being dyed.

Wetting-out

It is not sufficient to hold a skein under a tap or dip it in and out of a bowl of water. The fibres must be wet right through to the centre. Place the skeins in soft warm water for a few hours before dyeing so that the water can penetrate all the fibres. If a small amount of detergent is added to the water the wetting-out will be carried out more quickly. Before dyeing, rinse the yarn thoroughly and squeeze out the water evenly. Always make sure the yarn or raw material is evenly damp.

Bleaching

Occasionally wool is bleached before dyeing, but only when especially bright or pale clear shades are required. A very weak solution of hydrogen peroxide can be used.

Other animal fibres

If washing other animal fibres treat them as for wool, especially if they have a tendency to felt.

Silk

See page 71.

Vegetable fibres

Cotton and linen can stand rougher treatment than wool. They can be boiled and bleached as described in chapter 8, page 69.

Synthetic yarns

Man-made fibres are usually clean when received and only need a thorough wetting-out.

Water

The quality of water is of fundamental importance to the dyer.

Consider these questions about your water supply.

1 Is the water naturally hard or soft?

2 Is it acid, alkaline or neutral?

3 Is it the same every day?

4 Do you use a water softener?

Rain water is the purest form of natural water, but because of air pollution this may not be as pure as we would like. It can also collect impurities and particles of dust from roofs and gutters.

Water varies in its degree of acid, alkaline and mineral content, so these qualities will affect the colours resulting from the dye. Test the pH factor by using litmus paper (the pH factor is the measure of acidity or alkalinity). The numbers run from 0–14; 7 is neutral, over 7 denotes alkalinity, 7 downwards denotes acidity.

If the water is acidic add baking powder or borax until the reading is neutral. Only a small amount will be needed. If the water is alkaline add clear vinegar until the reading is neutral. Always test with a fresh piece of paper.

Hard water with a high mineral content could streak the yarn and cause irregular distribution of colour. It has the effect of dulling the colours obtained both during dyeing and washing. There is one exception: when dyeing with madder use hard water, or make soft water hard by adding a little powdered chalk. You will probably know whether the water is hard or soft from the way soap reacts when you wash your hands. It is easy to get a good lather with soft water, but with hard water the soap rinses off. The hardness of water is due to calcium and magnesium salts. Some types of hard water can be softened by boiling for 20–30 minutes or by adding water softener. If using water softeners add them before testing with litmus paper because the softener may affect the pH factor.

3
Methods of Dyeing

Natural dyestuffs can be divided into two groups: those which will produce a fast colour just by boiling, and those which need an additional chemical to make the colour permanent. The first group is known as substantive or non-mordant dyes, the second group adjective or mordant dyes.

A dyer will choose the type of dyestuff and method of dyeing to suit specific requirements. For someone who wishes to use dyestuff alone, there are a few substantive dyestuffs including walnuts and lichens. There may be dyers who object to the use of chemicals and are quite happy with colours which fade quickly; or perhaps when one colour has faded they like to apply another.

Walnuts and lichens have their own built-in acids, so the colours obtained from the dye-bath are fast. Some barks are reliable and certain roots are said to produce fast colours. Opinions vary about this, and individual experiments will be necessary to prove these points.

The chemicals (known as mordants) which are required to help make dyestuffs fast will be discussed in detail in the next chapter: it is one of the most important aspects in the dyeing of fast colours.

General instructions for using plants

This is the simplest basic recipe which can be used for wool. 120 g (4 oz) of wool is used throughout and 4.5 litres (1 gallon) of liquid for dyeing. Use any part of a plant which will produce a colour — flower heads, stems, leaves, berries, skin, bark, roots. As a rough guide, use equal quantities of dyestuff and material to be dyed.

1 Make sure the dyestuff is clean. Wash it in clear water.

2 Break up the material if necessary, i.e. chop leaves, crush berries, grind roots and bark.

3 If the dye source is hard, soak it overnight in soft water and use this water for dyeing. The dyestuff can be tied in a muslin or net bag.

4 Boil the dyestuff for about ½ hour.

5 There are now three choices: (a) Strain off the solid material and work with the remaining liquid. (b) Leave the dyestuff in the muslin bag while dyeing. (c) Leave the dyestuff loose in the liquid while dyeing. Make the dye-bath up to 4.5 litres (1 gallon) of liquid.

6 Have the yarn ready for dyeing. It should be clean and evenly damp.

7 Let the dye liquor cool and enter the wool.

Onion skins

Weld leaves

Dyeing yarn

8 Take about an hour to raise the liquor to the boil and then let it simmer for about half an hour. The time will vary according to depth of colour required.

9 After allowing the yarn to cool in the dye-bath lift it out with a smooth rod.

10 Rinse thoroughly in warm water and hang in the open air out of the sun, to dry.

Get into the habit of keeping records and samples of all colours. The basic recipe can be used for most natural dyestuffs. Cochineal, which is an insect, can be used in a similar way. Indigo and woad are exceptions, as their leaves will not give blue by boiling only.

Useful hints and practical suggestions

Muslin bags or net bags from the greengrocer's are useful for holding dyestuff or fleece.

Hard dye sources need boiling for a fairly long time for the colour to be extracted. Extract as much colour as possible before entering the wool. Yellow colouring matter can be spoilt by over-boiling, and turn dull and brownish.

If the dyestuff is likely to get mixed with the wool during dyeing it is better to keep it in a bag, or strain the liquid, for it can be very tedious separating the pieces. However, when the dyestuff is left loose in the bath the colour is often clearer and stronger. This is very evident with madder.

Before entering the wool allow the liquid to cool so that the clean, thoroughly wetted, wool does not suddenly get the shock of boiling dye-stuff. Take about an hour to raise the temperature to boiling point, then let the dye-bath simmer. The length of time for simmering will vary accord-

Removing skein from pan

This could encourage the dye to be uneven. When ready to rinse the yarn prepare plenty of water.

Rinsing
Rinsing is very important. It helps to set the colour and should remove loose dye. Try to avoid using sudden changes of temperature. Start with a warm rinse and use progressively colder ones. Rinsing water may need to be acid, alkaline, or neutral. In some cases, as with indigo, all three types of rinsing water are necessary.

Squeezing the yarn
The yarn can be squeezed from the top of the skein to the bottom or it can be lightly mangled or put through a wringer. A wringer with rubber rollers is ideal; a mangle with wooden rollers must be watched in case any dye is left on them.

Drying
A quick spin in a spin-drier is helpful. Put the skeins or fleece in an old pillowcase first. After spinning, shake the skeins, taking care not to tangle them, and hang them in the shade to dry. If they need a little tension, place weights on them.

After skeins have dried make sure they are labelled. If they are to be used at once place the skein on the back of a chair, a table swift or floor

Table swift which can be used vertically or horizontally. It opens to hold skeins of varying lengths

ing to the depth of colour required. An average time is from 30–60 minutes. Salt can be added to help exhaust the dyestuff.

Working the yarn
While the yarn is in the bath it should from time to time be gently moved with a clean, smooth, wooden, glass or stainless steel rod. Wooden rods become stained so glass or stainless steel rods are preferable.

If adding chemicals to the dye-bath always lift out the yarn on a stick before stirring them in.

Removing yarn from dye-bath
On the whole it is better to let the yarn cool in the dye-bath. Do not be tempted to lift out the yarn and leave it lying in a lump in a cold sink.

29

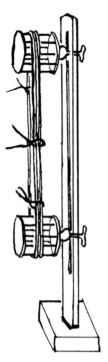

Floor swift which can be adjusted to hold skeins of different lengths

swift (skein holder). If you have chosen a thicker yarn for the four tied loops it will be easy to find them. Make sure they will slip round; sometimes a length is pulled out of place, but if the skein is well shaken this should not happen. Having made sure the ties will all move freely, remove them carefully. Lastly, cut the thread tied to the beginning and end of the skein. The yarn is now ready to be wound into balls or bobbins.

Check that your records are complete. It is very difficult to remember exact details after a few days.

The recipes which follow are for walnuts and lichen. These dyes produce fast colours without the use of mordants.

A typical experiment using walnuts (a substantive dye)

120 g (4 oz) of clean wool divided into four skeins
30 walnut hulls
4.5 litres (1 gallon) soft water for the dye-bath

Steep the hulls overnight in soft water if they are freshly picked. If they have been stored in water for some months just bring them to the boil. (When green walnuts are picked they can be placed in a screw-top jar filled with water and kept in a dark place for future use). After boiling the liquid for about 1 hour the walnuts can be discarded and the liquor cooled. This is to avoid putting wool into boiling dye. Make sure there are 4.5 litres (1 gallon) of liquid in the dye-bath before entering the clean, thoroughly wetted, wool. Gently move the skeins around to help the dye penetrate the fibres evenly, but do not agitate the skeins unduly. The dye-bath can be stirred well before the yarn is immersed but after the yarn is in the dye, stir as little as possible. In fact 'stir' is not a good word to use: *move* the wool gently. This movement is usually described by the word *work*. 'Working' the wool means gently moving it under the liquor using a clean, smooth, wooden rod or glass rod. Gradually bring the dye-bath to the boil and then let it simmer. Take the four skeins out at ten-minute intervals so that they will have been in the dye-bath 10 minutes, 20 minutes, 30 minutes and 40 minutes. Each one should be darker than the last. When removing a skein let it drain over the dye-bath, then rinse in hot soft water, squeeze and rinse in warm clear water. Label the skein and hang it in the shade to dry.

Dyeing with lichen

Lichen is a fascinating plant to study; there is still a great deal to be discovered about its valuable properties. An alga and a fungus combine to make lichen, and these two organisms grow in mutual relationship (symbiosis). Lichen can be found on rocks, walls, roofs, trees, tombstones, concrete and pavements, but it is sensitive to pollution such as sulphur dioxide, oil and radio-active fall-out. It came as a shock to me at first when I moved to the industrial part of West Yorkshire and could not find lichen, as there had always been so much in the Sussex countryside. In 1890 80 different lichens were identified in Sutton Park (near Birmingham) but the number has been greatly reduced as a result of pollution in the atmosphere. It has been possible to find as many as 150 species of lichen in some churchyards in the south-east of England. Lichens can stand great extremes of temperature and are found in deserts and tundra.

Lichen is sometimes associated with Scotland and Harris tweed, for the familiar brown, tan and gold colours were once obtained from lichen which grew on the rocks in the Hebrides. They left a pleasant aroma on the wool which reminded one of a walk through the woods. In a dye-house the smell from a lichen dye-pot is always unmistakable.

When looking for lichen, do not collect rare species, for they take a long time to grow. If there is a plentiful supply in the woods a small amount can be collected without doing any harm.

It is easier to collect lichen after rain — carefully scrape it from the surface with a knife. Shake it free from grit or if it was collected from a tree, remove pieces of bark. The bark could darken the colour if left in by mistake. On the other hand, if a darker colour is required the bark could serve a useful purpose. Lichen can be dried and used at any time.

There are two ways of obtaining colour from lichen, but each method does not necessarily work with every species. Lichens can be boiled, or fermented first and then boiled. Some lichens will respond to each method, producing one colour as a result of boiling and a different one after fermenting.

Lichens contain acids, which can eat away the rock on which they are growing. It is these acids which apparently give a range of colours, including yellow, tan, brown, pink, orange, red, magenta, purple and occasionally blue. As the acid content is affected by light, lichens chosen from sunny situations after a fine summer usually give better results. The acids are colourless. In order to find out if a plant contains *orciene* (the colourless acid necessary for producing orchil) it must be tested with an alkali. Shake a little of the powdered plant in a glass with a solution of water and ammonia. Seal the glass for a day or two; if the liquid turns purple the lichen will yield a purple dye.

I have chosen five lichens to illustrate the two methods of extracting colour. *Parmelia saxatilis* and *Parmelia omphalodes* will give reddish-brown by boiling, *Ochrolechia tartarea* will give purple after fermentation, *Xanthoria parietina* and *Evernia prunastri* will give purplish-red by fermenting and a yellowish colour after boiling.

Parmelia saxatilis (*crottle*)

This lichen is common throughout Britain, Scandinavia and the USA. It forms flat, grey rosettes of rather narrow lobes. The surface is covered with a fine network of white lines. Short greyish-brown, rod-like outgrowths develop in the centres of older plants. It was used for dyeing Harris tweed in shades of brown.

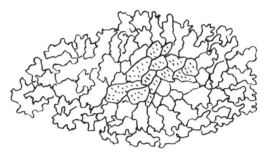

Parmelia saxatilis (crottle)

Parmelia omphalodes (*black crottle*)

This lichen grows rather loosely attached to rocks in mountainous districts. The bluntly tipped lobes are often reddish-brown with a purplish glint. It is found in Britain, Scandinavia and the USA. It grows at higher altitudes than the other parmelias. Reddish-brown is obtained by the boiling method.

Parmelia omphalodes (black crottle)

Ochrolechia tartarea (*cudbear*)

This lichen forms thick grey crusts with irregular, rough and lumpy surfaces on rocks and also on the bark of trees in upland districts of Britain, Scandinavia and parts of the USA. Scottish and Welsh crofters used to steep it in urine for many weeks and then make it up into balls with lime or chalk and hang them up to dry. Cudbear was being manufactured in Scotland in 1758.

Ochrolechia tartarea (cudbear)

Evernia prunastri

This is a common lichen found on trees and fences. It has flattened branches which fork several times. The upper surface is greenish-grey, the under surface white. It grows all over Britain and in the temperate zones of the USA.

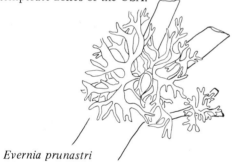

Evernia prunastri

Xanthoria parietina

This lichen is very common; it is found on trees, walls and roofs. It has deep yellow or orange lobes and the spore-producing apothecia are a deeper shade of the same colour.

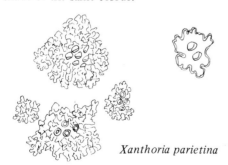

Xanthoria parietina

Boiling water methods

These are for use with *parmelia saxatilis* or *parmelia omphalodes*. Lichen can be packed into a dye-bath without being tied in muslin for it can easily be shaken out of the wool. As lichen swells when in water make sure the dye-bath is big enough.

Bruise the lichen well when it is wet, but if it is dry squeeze it in the hand to crack it. Do not wash the lichens in case the acids are washed away by mistake. Remember to pick out bark and moss.

Method 1

1 Allow equal quantities of wool and lichen.

2 Bring lichen slowly to the boil in soft water.

3 Let it simmer for about 3 hours and leave the dye overnight.

4 Next day, enter the well-wetted wool and simmer until the colour is satisfactory.

5 When the liquid is cold, remove the wool, wash and rinse it.

Method 2

1 Arrange alternate layers of lichen and wool until the pot is nearly full.

2 Add soft water to cover the lichen.

3 Heat the pot and let it simmer for several hours. This process can be repeated the next day if a darker colour is required.

Method 3

The colour can be extracted from the lichen as in the first three stages of Method 1, the liquid strained and then used.

It will be noted that Method 2 requires less heat than the other two methods. NB: A little acetic acid added to the dye-bath will help extract the colour.

Fermentation

In order to obtain orchil acid, the lichen must be fermented with ammonia, water and oxygen in a warm atmosphere. Keep the temperature between 15° and 24°C; a sunny window-sill, greenhouse or airing cupboard would be suitable places. Stir the mixture from time to time.

Recipe for Ochrolechia tartarea (cudbear lichen)

1 Rub the dried lichen through a sieve and make sure other vegetable matter has been removed.

2 Place powdered lichen in a jar and add the ammonia solution. This should consist of 1 part household ammonia and 2 parts water.

3 Put a lid on the jar and put it in a warm place.

4 Stir five or six times a day until the colour runs, and then stir less frequently. Keep the lid on to prevent the ammonia from escaping. The liquid will form a purplish-red and be ready after 15–28 days.

This dye can be used straight away. One tablespoonful will dye about 60 g (2 oz) of wool or the liquid can be evaporated and the dried dye stored for future use. When using this dye, experiment by adding a little soda to one dye-bath and some acetic acid to another. One colour will probably tend to be a bluish-purple, while the other will be a reddish-purple.

Boiling and fermenting

Xanthoria parietina is easily obtained: it grows on walls and in farmyards. When using one of the boiling methods the resulting colour will be yellowish-tan. After fermentation, the boiling method plus a little soda will give purplish-red.

In *Lichens for Vegetable Dyeing* Eileen Bolton describes how she obtained blue from this second method by leaving the wool in the dye-bath in a warm place for two to four weeks and then squeezing it and putting it outside in brilliant sunshine. Long boiling, long steeping and brilliant sun were all necessary for a successful blue.

Evernia prunastri can be boiled or fermented. It gives an orchil from the evernic acid and pale yellow from another acid, atranorine. The plant is used by perfumiers as a fixative for other ingredients. I have read that in Poland the plant is protected by law and may only be gathered from felled trees (*Flowerless Plants*, Oxford University Press).

Roccella tinctoria (*orchil*)

From a historical point of view this lichen is very interesting. It is found on the rocks of many Mediterranean islands and in the Canary Islands.

It grows upright with single and double stems about 5 cm (2 in.) high. When mature these stems are crowned with round or flat formations. A dark red paste is made from these heads. For many years the method of obtaining this paste was kept secret. Orseille or orchil was the most important lichen dye used by ancient and medieval dyers. The beautiful purple shade was used as a preliminary dye, to 'give ground'.

Orchil acid is contained in a number of lichens and it is known by different names, e.g. in Italy it is oricello, in Spain orcigilia, in France orseille, in Portugal urzela, and in England orchal, archil or orchil.

4
Mordanting

The Chinese had dye workshops in 3000 BC. The first western dyers are thought to have been the primitive lake dwellers of the area now known as Switzerland, in around 2000 BC. As a result of the dry air in the Egyptian tombs which preserves cloth, it is apparent that mordants, chemicals which help to make colours permanent, were definitely used between 2200 and 1500 BC.

It is impossible to know exactly how dyers first discovered that mordants would make their colours fast, but there are still many people today who have the knowledge to adapt ingredients around them and turn them into useful mordants. Wood ash, salt, vinegar, oak galls, urine and certain plants, roots and barks have been used to fix colours. The baths in which wool is dyed have often been chosen for the effect they have on the colour. Cast iron pots plus rusty nails darken colours, brass pots can help to obtain brighter results; an aluminium pot with baking soda also brightens colours.

According to Pliny, the Egyptians had a method of using different mordants on one piece of cloth, so that after dyeing in one bath the material was dyed in a number of permanent colours.

It is interesting to imagine how the early dyers discovered that certain chemicals would fix colours. Wood ash gives valuable chemicals; perhaps rotting leaves or pieces of bark became mixed with wood ash and stained fibres or skin. Those early users of indigo who found out how to turn the green leaves of the *indigofera tinctoria* into a beautiful blue dye made an important discovery, as did those who could obtain Tyrian purple from shell fish and magenta from unpromising lichen.

The majority of natural dyes need a chemical in the form of a metal salt to create an affinity between the fibre and the pigment. These chemicals are known as *mordants*, the name being derived from the Latin *mordere*, to bite. It was thought at one time that the mordants ate away the surface of the fibre so that the dye could sink in. It was the general opinion that the metallic salts, because of their corrosive nature, made the textiles rough, opened their pores and made them more receptive to the colouring matters. A mordant is now regarded as a chemical which can itself be fixed on the fibre and which also combines with the dyestuff. A

Four mordants

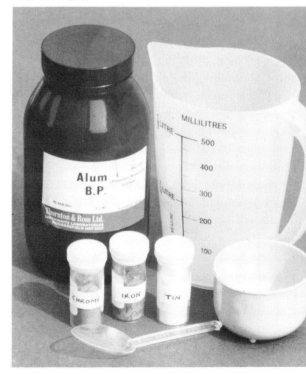

link is therefore formed between dyestuff and fibre which allows certain colours with no affinity for the fibre to be fixed. Where the colours are capable of being dyed directly, the mordant helps to produce faster shades by forming an insoluble compound of mordant and dyestuff within the fibre itself. For example, some people use mordants with substantive dyes such as lichen or walnuts. In these cases the mordant is not needed to make the dye fast, but it can alter the colour to a certain extent.

Chemical mordants

These four mordants are in general use:

Alum Potassium aluminium sulphate – obtainable in the form of white crystals. This is a popular and safe mordant to use.

Chrome Potassium dichromate – sold in the form of orange crystals. It is sensitive to light. This is the most modern mordant and is widely used.

Iron Ferrous sulphate, copperas, green vitriol – can be obtained as soft green crystals.

Tin Stannous chloride – sold as off-white crystals. This mordant must be used carefully and sparingly.

Mordanting can be carried out at different stages in the dyeing process:

1 Before dyeing

2 During dyeing

3 Simultaneously (mordant put in at beginning with dye)

4 After dyeing (as in the case of iron)

5 Before and after dyeing

The choice of time and method will sometimes depend on one's own preference, but often the required colour will demand a certain procedure. On the whole I prefer to mordant first so that I can judge the type of colour and strength of dye to be prepared. Mordanting must be carried out accurately, whereas dyeing allows for greater freedom. Do not hurry over mordanting; successful dyeing depends on thorough mordanting.

If a tin mordant is added during dyeing this is done to brighten a colour, whereas the addition of iron would darken or 'sadden' the colour. Iron can be fairly difficult to use for it can make the colour uneven and patchy.

The colour should be well and truly fixed if the fifth method is used. In this case the wool would probably be mordanted in alum first and then, after dyeing, one of the other three chemical mordants would be used to give different effects. Terms used to describe the effects of mordants are 'blooming', when tin is added to brighten the colour, and 'saddening' when iron is used to darken the colour.

Copper sulphate, a mordant used less frequently, can be added to change a colour. For example, if it is used on wool which has been mordanted in alum and dyed with horsetails, yellow wool will turn light green.

Preparation of skeins

It is very important that skeins should be tied properly before washing, mordanting and dyeing (see page 24). Much valuable information can be contained in the ties which are attached to the skeins. It is useful to have information which is readily available because samples cannot always be mounted at once. If the skeins have been prepared for washing they will have the following ties:

1 A strong thread taken round the beginning and end of the yarn

2 Strong threads in about four places round the hank

The knot system now has to be introduced in order to identify the mordants used. First of all I abbreviate the names of the mordants and think of them in alphabetical order: alum, chrome, iron, tin. Alum always has one knot, chrome two knots, iron three knots and tin four knots. The knots can be tied on a separate thread (B) on the end of the hank (A), or in two places (A) and (C) (see diagram).

Dye liquor ratio

This term describes the amount of liquor which a given weight of material needs in order to be satisfactorily worked. Too much liquor can be

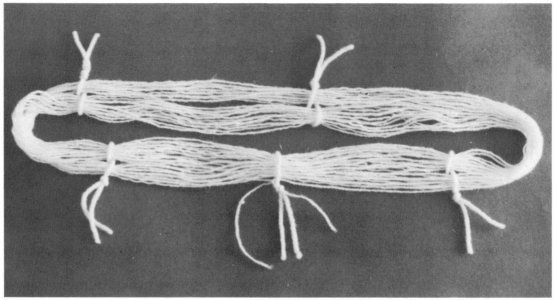

Skein ready for mordanting

wasteful, whereas insufficient will lead to uneven penetration of dye or mordant.

Work out beforehand how much liquid is required so that the right size of bath can be chosen. Experienced dyers would probably work with a ratio of 20:1 (weight in grams: liquor in litres), but it is advisable for beginners to work with a 30:1 or 40:1 liquor ratio. If working with a 30:1 liquor ratio use at least:

1 litre (1.75 pints) of liquid for 30 g (1 oz) of yarn

4 litres (7 pints) of liquid for 120 g (4 oz) of yarn

16 litres (28 pints) of liquid for 480 g (1 lb) of yarn

The mordanting process

Make sure the fibres are wet right through to the middle and that they are evenly damp. This is called 'wetting-out'. Yarn should be moved gently, not stirred round in a circular movement. It can be moved by turning with a clean, smooth rod or stick. Make sure stirring rods are suitably long and strong. Try to have some way of preventing them from slipping into the bath. Glass rods could be bent in a right-angle at the end; a wire could be passed through the end of a wooden rod and bent over the dye-bath or over the handle.

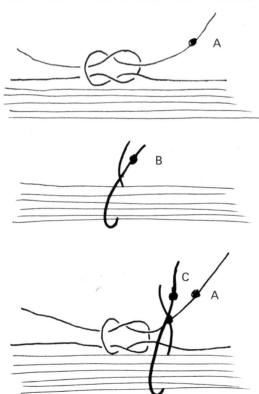

Tie knots for identifying mordants at A or B, or A and C

Potassium aluminium sulphate (alum)

Use materials which are clean and evenly damp. Skeins should be correctly tied. Remember the identification knots or threads.

Mordanting with alum

Skein has been tied, wetted-out and squeezed

Alum and cream of tartar dissolved in boiling water

Dissolved mordant stirred into heated bath. Skein entered

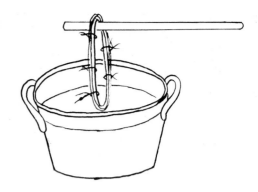

Skein lifted from bath

Recipe

120 g (4 oz) clean wetted-out wool
30 g (1 oz) alum (slightly less for pale shades)
7 g (¼ oz) cream of tartar
4.5 litres (1 gallon) of soft water

1 Heat the soft water to approximately 30°C.

2 Dissolve alum and cream of tartar in a small pot of boiling water.

3 Add the solution of alum and cream of tartar to the bath and stir well.

4 Enter the clean, thoroughly wetted-out wool.

5 Bring the liquid slowly to the boil. Take about an hour over this stage. Coarse wool will need a little longer than fine wool.

6 Gently turn the wool over once or twice to make sure it is evenly distributed in the liquid. Every part of the skein must be thoroughly mordanted.

7 When boiling point has been reached, lower the heat and simmer for about an hour at 95°C. Turn the wool once more, making sure it is below the level of the liquid.

Effect on wool: the wool does not change colour.

After this stage the dyer has three choices:

1 (a) Allow the yarn to cool in the bath to 35°C.
(b) Lift the wool out with a stick and let it drain.
(c) Remove excess liquid by squeezing the hank downwards.
(d) Store skeins in this damp condition for a day

37

or two. They can be wrapped in a towel or kept in a pillowcase. Yarn in this damp condition will be evenly wetted-out and in a good state for dyeing.

or

2 Leave the yarn in the liquor all night, then after removing it in the morning squeeze gently to remove excess liquid. Do not wash the wool, but prepare to dye it at once.

or

3 Allow the yarn to dry completely. Label and store for future use.

It is perfectly satisfactory to mordant yarn and store it in this condition, but it will have to be thoroughly wetted-out before dyeing.

Potassium dichromate (bichromate of potash) (chrome)

As chrome is sensitive to light, take precautions to keep the yarn away from the light.

Recipe
120 g (4 oz) clean wetted-out wool
3.5 g ($\frac{1}{8}$ oz) potassium dichromate (less for paler shades)
4.5 litres (1 gallon) soft water

1 Heat the soft water to approximately 30°C.

2 Dissolve chrome in a small pot of boiling water.

3 Add this solution to the bath and stir well. The liquid will appear golden.

4 Enter the clean, thoroughly wetted-out wool.

5 Keep the yarn completely submerged by placing a weight or a plate on it.

6 Cover the bath with a lid and take about an hour to bring the liquid to the boil.

7 Turn the wool carefully once or twice, taking care to keep it away from the light.

8 Simmer for about an hour at 95°C. Turn the wool once more. The time taken over this stage will vary according to the type of wool. Coarse wool requires 1–1½ hours; fine wool ¾–1 hour.

9 Remove from heat and allow the yarn to cool to 35°C so that it can be handled safely.

10 Rinse yarn, away from the light, in water of similar temperature.

11 Squeeze the wool evenly and place in a covered bowl or towel.

Effect on wool: it turns pale golden.

There are two reasons for trying to dye this wool at once: (a) it will be evenly wetted-out; (b) it will not have the chance to be affected by light. If dyeing is delayed, dry the wool and store it in the dark until it is needed, remembering to attach a label giving mordanting details. 6 g ($\frac{1}{5}$ oz) of cream of tartar can be added to the bath: this adds brilliancy to the colours and can alter the tints.

There are three main ways of using chrome:

1 Mordant in chrome, remove the wool and dye in a second bath which has already been prepared with dyestuff.

or

2 Dye the wool first, then add chrome to the dye-bath (after removing the wool), or after dyeing prepare a separate bath with chrome mordant only – this is called 'after chroming'.

or

3 Dye and mordant simultaneously.

Generally, one of these methods is found to be suitable for each dyestuff. Experiment and decide which method gives the best results. In many cases chrome has replaced iron. It is a popular mordant and helps to produce fast colours. Chrome can be safely used on nylon. Because of its chemical constitution, the dyeing properties of nylon are similar to those of wool and silk. Wool, when it has been mordanted in chrome, feels soft and silky.

Additional points concerning chrome
Chrome is a very useful and pleasant mordant to use but it must be handled carefully. Always measure amounts accurately, taking care not to spill any of the crystals.

Chrome is very sensitive to light and, if dyeing is to be even, this fact must be remembered throughout the mordanting and dyeing process. Keep chrome in the dark, in a dark jar. Wool in the mordanted state is sensitive to the action of light: the unexposed mordanted wool has a yellowish colour but when exposed to the light it becomes greenish, through reduction of the absorbed salt and deposition of chromic oxide. These exposed and unexposed portions will behave differently in the dye-bath. The unexposed part dyes more rapidly than the exposed and appears darker and less brilliant. It may be that the exposed portion dyes more slowly because it is less absorbent.

When mordanting, keep the wool submerged. Only remove the lid while gently turning the wool.

After taking the wool out of the mordant, keep it away from the light by keeping it covered in a bath or wrapped in a towel.

If wool has been mordanted with alum, a small amount of chrome can be added to a dye-bath towards the end of dyeing in order to add depth to a colour.

Chrome is a mordant which is widely used commercially. Some nylon for ladies' underwear is mordanted in chrome and dyed with logwood chips and fustic. This colour does not change in artificial light.

Ferrous sulphate (also known as copperas or green vitriol) (iron)

Iron is a very useful mordant but it can be difficult to use as it has a tendency to make the colour uneven. Try to keep a bath exclusively for this mordant.

Wool is usually dyed first and then mordanted with iron. The colour is always darkened by the addition of iron — this is known as 'saddening'.

Recipe

120 g (4 oz) clean wetted-out wool
3.5 g ($\frac{1}{8}$ oz) ferrous sulphate (less for pale shades)
7 g (¼ oz) cream of tartar
4.5 litres (1 gallon) soft water

1 Dye the yarn in the chosen colour for 45 minutes.

2 Dissolve the iron and cream of tartar in a small pot of hot water.

3 Turn off heat and lift the yarn from the dye-bath with a rod.

4 Add the dissolved mordant to the bath and stir thoroughly.

5 Re-enter the yarn and work for five minutes.

6 Turn on heat and raise liquor to the boil.

7 Continue dyeing at 95°C for about 20 minutes. During this time occasionally move the yarn gently in order to make a level colour.

8 Rinse yarn thoroughly after using iron. This is essential to avoid the wool being made tender. Iron can make the wool feel hard.

Effect on wool: it turns pale fawn if mordanted before dyeing.

Many subtle shades are obtained with an iron mordant. They form a valuable part of a colour scheme and can be used to enhance the bright colours obtained from wool mordanted in alum or tin.

Additional points concerning iron

The temperature of the mordanting bath must be raised very gradually so that the dyeing will be even. Lower the wool all at once into the bath, otherwise the first part of the skein will absorb more mordant than the rest. On the other hand, if an unevenly dyed skein is required, mordant irregularly.

If wool which has been mordanted in iron is to be dyed in the same bath as other yarns, make sure that the wool has been thoroughly rinsed. The slightest trace of iron will dull other colours. I saw the results of inadequate rinsing when four skeins were dyed in fustic chips: instead of coming from the dye-bath in four shades of yellow ranging from very bright with a tin mordant to dull olive from iron, they were all dull with very little variation.

Stannous chloride (tin)

Tin crystals used as a mordant can have a dramatic effect on colour. They must be used carefully for they could almost destroy the wool if weighed incorrectly.

It is possible to mordant first, during dyeing, or near the end of dyeing. Different colour changes occur according to the time chosen to mordant.
For each method:
120g (4 oz) clean wetted-out wool
3.5 g ($\frac{1}{8}$ oz) stannous chloride
3.5 g ($\frac{1}{8}$ oz) cream of tartar or oxalic acid
4.5 litres (1 gallon) of soft water

Method 1 – Mordanting first

1 Heat soft water in mordanting-bath to 30°C.

2 Dissolve tin crystals in a small pot of warm water.

3 Dissolve cream of tartar or oxalic acid in a separate pot of boiling water and add these to the mordant bath. Stir well.

4 Add the dissolved tin crystals. Stir well.

5 Enter the well-wetted wool.

6 Bring the liquid slowly to the boil. Take about an hour for this, turning the wool at least once.

7 Simmer for one hour at 95°C.

8 Allow yarn to cool in the mordanting-bath.

9 When the wool can be handled rinse it well in warm, slightly soapy water.

10 Rinse again in clear water, squeeze out excess water and dye as soon as possible.

Effect on wool: it does not change colour.

Method 2 – Mordanting during dyeing

This method is usually used to obtain scarlet with cochineal.

1 Follow Method 1 from 1 to 4.

5 Add the required amount of dyestuff.

6 Enter the well-wetted wool and continue to dye and mordant at the same time. The depth of colour required will determine the length of time taken over this stage.

7 Allow the yarn to cool in the dye-bath, then rinse very thoroughly, first in warm soapy water and finally in clear water.

Method 3 – Mordanting near the end of dyeing

This method is used for brightening a colour, usually on wool which has been mordanted with alum. It is known as 'blooming'.

Dye the yarn to within 20 minutes of its allotted time.

1 Dissolve the tin crystals in a small pot of warm water, and the cream of tartar or oxalic acid in a separate small pot of boiling water.

2 Twenty minutes before the dyeing has been completed turn off the heat from the dye-bath.

3 Lift out the yarn, then add dissolved cream of tartar or oxalic acid. Stir well.

4 Add dissolved tin crystals. Stir well.

5 Replace yarn, gently stir it around in the liquid for five minutes.

6 Raise to the boil and then simmer at 95°C. This should take about 20 minutes, but watch the colour so that the yarn can be removed when the required brightness has been developed.

7 Rinse the yarn in warm soapy water.

8 Rinse in clear water.

Additional points concerning tin

If too much tin is used it can make the fibres harsh, and spinning could be a little more difficult. The fleece also appears coarser. Because of these possible problems wool was often dyed scarlet in the form of cloth rather than as loose wool or yarn.

Take great care not to confuse alum and tin, for at least eight times as much alum is required for mordanting. One of my pupils mistook tin for alum with the result that the wool disintegrated and pulled apart in our hands after mordanting. Some dyers use oxalic acid instead of cream of tartar, but I prefer cream of tartar, which avoids the use of a poisonous chemical.

Assistants

Assistants are those substances which are of use to the dyer but cannot be classed as colouring matters, mordants or fixing agents.

Acetic acid

This is also known in its dilute and less pure form as vinegar. Dye-bath solutions are acidified with it and it is used to neutralize calcareous water.

Cream of tartar

This white crystalline substance is used in conjunction with mordants. It brightens colours.

Sodium sulphate

This is known as Glauber's salt and is used extensively by wool dyers to obtain even, regular or level dyeing. Glauber's salt can help to regulate the rapidity with which wool takes up the colour.

Boiled-off liquor

This is the soapy liquid which has been used when

removing silk-glue from raw silk before dyeing. It is slightly alkaline and can serve the same purpose for the silk dyer as sodium sulphate does for the wool dyer. It causes the colouring matter to be attracted more slowly and evenly by the silk and helps to preserve the lustre. Too much is injurious – it wastes colouring matter and destroys the lustre of the silk. Suggested quantities are 50–100 ml (1.7–3.5 fl.oz) of boiled off liquor to 1 litre of dye-bath solution.

General hints on mordanting

I consider that mordanting is the most important part of dyeing. If this process is not carried out in a thorough way, resulting colours can be a great disappointment; they may be uneven, patchy or unstable. If the yarn has been inadequately mordanted the ultimate colour could be dull, it would be liable to rub off and the wool might feel harsh and unpleasant. As well as helping to make the colour fast, the mordant has a great influence on resulting colours, particularly the polygenetic colours such as those obtained from logwood chips and madder.

Always weigh mordants accurately and see that they are thoroughly dissolved in water before being added to the mordanting bath.

Alum
This mordant is not difficult to use, but if too much is mixed in the bath it will make the wool feel sticky and stringy, and it will appear to lose some of its elasticity.

Chrome
Always take care to keep the solution and the mordanted wool away from the light. If dyeing loose wool this is not so important as when dyeing yarn, because uneven loose wool can be carded together. Too much chrome could spoil the colours.

Iron
Keep a separate bath for iron if possible because it is difficult to clean pans after mordanting and the slightest trace of iron could dull other colours. If stainless steel pans are being used the problem of cleaning will be solved. I prefer to keep a pan just for iron mordanting. Try to lower the wool in all at once. Too much iron would quickly harden the wool.

Tin
This mordant must be measured very carefully. Too much tin will destroy wool, making it harsh, brittle and unrecognizable.

Group work

If mordanting and dyeing are to be introduced to a group in school or at a Guild meeting it is advisable to make sure the organization is well planned beforehand. Individuals should try to grasp the basic essentials, but their time will probably be limited. Successful dyeing cannot usually be hurried. For recipes, see chapter 6.

Preliminary preparation
1 Choose clean yarn so that it only has to be wetted-out.

2 Weigh out the correct amount of mordants beforehand.

3 Four clean stainless steel pans should be ready for the mordants.

4 A means of heating four pans at once will be required.

5 Soak fustic chips and logwood chips.

Working arrangements for 16 people
1 Each person to be given a skein to tie in readiness for mordanting.

2 Four people to be responsible for each mordant, so they will tie the identification knots according to the plan of one for alum, two for chrome, three for iron and four for tin.

3 Mordants will be mixed and mordanting baths prepared by one member of each group.

4 Yarns will be thoroughly wetted-out and immersed in the mordants.

5 While the yarns are being mordanted four dye-baths can be prepared.

On an occasion like this, it will be advisable to choose strong colours which will give a fairly

Mordanting in a group

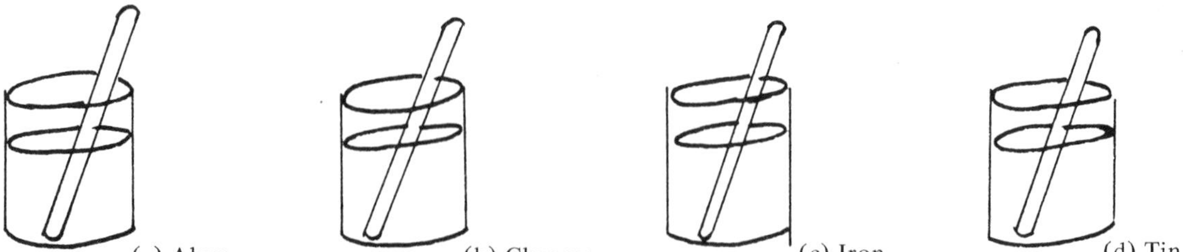

(a) Alum (b) Chrome (c) Iron (d) Tin

Four mordants accurately weighed and dissolved

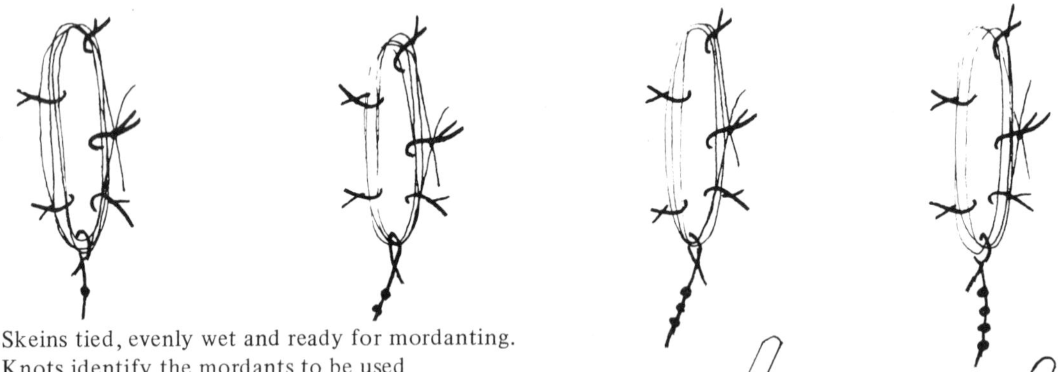

Skeins tied, evenly wet and ready for mordanting.
Knots identify the mordants to be used

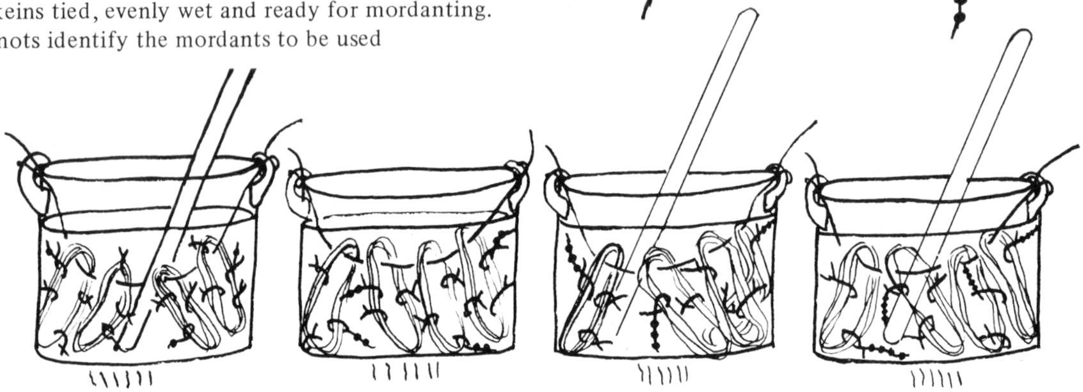

Mordants have been added to pans. Four skeins in
each pan. Use a lid on the second pan from the left

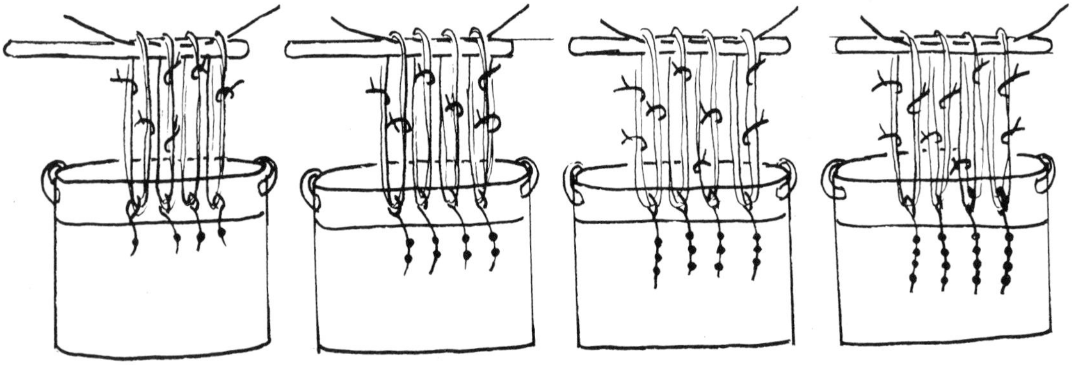

Lifting skeins from pans

42

quick result. Fustic chips, madder, logwood and cochineal would be particularly suitable.

6 Lift the skeins from the mordant baths, taking care to rinse according to the recipes. Emphasize the need to rinse the iron-mordanted wool well, so that it does not dull the other colours.

7 Place into each dye-bath four skeins, each one having been mordanted in a different mordant. Leave these until the desired colour is obtained.

Remember to tie a different thread on each group to identify the dye.

8 Remove skeins from dye-baths, rinse them well and examine the resulting colours. The effect of the different mordants should be very obvious when the wool is dry.

9 Each person can make a colour chart after sharing out the 16 samples.

Using four dyes

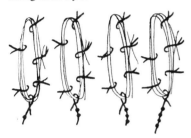

Take a skein from each mordant

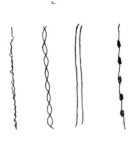

Use a different fibre to identify each dye

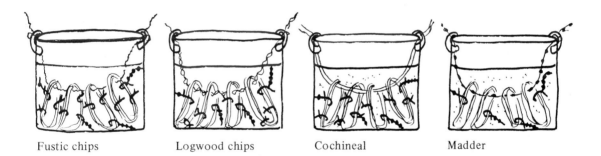

Fustic chips   Logwood chips   Cochineal   Madder

A typical colour chart

	Fustic chips	Madder	Logwood	Cochineal
Alum	Bright yellow	Vermilion	Bluish-purple	Purplish-red
Chrome	Gold	Brick red	Dark blue	Purplish-crimson
Iron	Olive yellow	Chocolate	Almost black	Dull red
Tin	Clear yellow	Orange	Purple	Scarlet

This is a basic chart; within the plan one could work with fleece, combed tops, a variety of fibres or different kinds of cloth. There would still be some dye left, so other experiments could be made — lighter colours could be obtained and dyes could be mixed together in different proportions. Notes should be kept throughout the experiments.

43

5
Adjective Dyes

This chapter describes a selection of dyestuffs which require mordants to make the colours permanent. The suggestions are meant as a guide and should lead to other experiments. Assume that the wool has already been mordanted.

The dyestuffs are placed into seven groups according to the part which has been used. It is advisable to use equal quantities of dyestuff and yarn, but amounts can be altered as a result of individual experiments.

1 Bark

2 Roots

3 Flowers

4 Flowers, leaves and stems

5 Leaves and stalks

6 Skins

7 Berries

Bark

When using bark, cut it into small pieces and soak thoroughly in order to help extract colour before boiling.

Alder (Alnus glutinosa)
The alder is the most common waterside tree in the British Isles. It usually grows on the banks of rivers, lakes and marshes from the lowlands of eastern England up to 500 metres (1500 ft) in the Scottish Highlands. The name alder comes from the Anglo-Saxon *aler* and is a common element in place names, for example Aldershot means alder wood. It has a black fissured bark and broad unpointed, dull green leaves. Catkins appear in autumn and develop in spring.

The leaves can be boiled for a yellow dye, but the bark is particularly useful as it will produce brown to black shades according to the length of time it is boiled.

Method
Steep the bark overnight. Heat this liquor slowly and simmer. After straining the bark and cooling the liquid, enter the clean, wetted yarn. Black will be obtained if a teaspoonful of iron and half a teaspoonful of copper sulphate are added before dyeing is completed. Rinse very thoroughly. Resulting colour: iron mordant – black.

English Oak (Quercus robur)
English Oak grows in hedges and woods throughout England especially on the heavy soils in the Midlands and South. If you can find some oak trees which have been felled, strip the bark away from the trunk and take out the soft inner bark.

It is possible to use unmordanted wool as well as mordanted wool because the tannin in the bark helps to make the colour fast.

Method
Heat the bark slowly and then let it simmer for 1½ hours. Strain the liquid and allow to cool. Enter the clean wetted-out wool. Bring to the boil and then simmer for about 1 hour. Rinse the wool thoroughly and dry.
Resulting colours:

No mordant	– light warm brown, dark honey
Alum	– yellow
Chrome	– gold
Iron	– dull olive
Tin	– golden orange

Many other barks can be used to produce a col-

Bloodroot (*Sanguinaria canadensis*)

lection of very attractive shades, which will usually range from cream, fawn, tan, brown, reddish-brown to black. Try using bark from apple, cherry and willow trees.

Roots

Roots need careful preparation. After being selected and dug up they have to be washed and thoroughly dried before being ground or chopped up.

The quality of the colour obtained from roots varies according to the weather of the previous season as well as the present one. The roots will contain less dye if there is little sun or if the summer is too dry. Usually the dye is stronger in the roots if they are gathered before flowering.

Bloodroot (Sanguinaria canadensis)
This flower is found in North America and in British gardens. It has white flowers and blooms in April and May. Seonaid Robertson in her book

Dyes from Plants suggests that the Ojibwa dyed their porcupine quills red with this dye.

Method
Cut the roots into small pieces and soak overnight. Use this water in the dye-bath. Place the roots in a muslin bag or plastic net along with the wetted-out wool. Raise the temperature, and simmer the wool and roots for about ½ hour.
Resulting colours:

Alum	— red-orange
Chrome	— gold-orange
Iron	— warm khaki
Tin	— pinkish-red

William Robertson grew some fine plants in his garden in Dundee, as the photograph shows.

Anchusa or alkanet (Anchusa tinctoria)
There are many forms of anchusa or alkanet, belonging to the Borage family. The plants grow wild in Britain and Europe; in gardens they are cultivated for their beautiful blue flowers. The

45

plant has an erect hairy stem with hairy leaves and grows to about a metre (3 ft) in height. The roots were used for a red dye but it is not easy to obtain good strong colours from the plants grown in gardens, and the flowers are so beautiful that they are likely to give more pleasure than the rather disappointing red which may be obtained from their roots. It is possible to buy prepared extract.

Method
Prepare the dye-bath by boiling the roots or using the extract. Cool the liquor, enter the clean well-wetted wool and simmer for about ½ hour. After drying the wool without rinsing, give it an alkaline afterbath to bring out the blue colour or an acid bath to accentuate the red shade. Use 2 tablespoons of ammonia for the alkaline afterbath and three tablespoons of acetic acid for the acid afterbath in 3 litres (5 pints) of water. Rinse the wool thoroughly and then dry.
Resulting colour: light red.

Lady's bedstraw (Galium verum)
This is a sprawling plant which smells of hay. It is found in grassy places throughout Europe and North America. At one time people used to sleep on mattresses of dried bedstraw and other plants. They smelt pleasant and could be burned and renewed when soiled. The roots provide a red dye which was popular in the Hebrides and used for the red in tartans. It is not advisable to dig up these roots and rob the countryside of the flowers, but it is interesting to know how the colour was obtained.

Method
The roots were dug up and washed thoroughly, and they were then chopped up into small pieces, heated slowly and simmered. Clean wetted wool was entered in the usual way.
Resulting colours: light red to pink.

Try also dock roots and roots of the yellow flag iris for black dyes.

Flowers

The majority of flowers will give different shades of yellow and yellowish-green. Wallflower petals and yellow pansies have been known to give clear greens. When the East Sussex Guild of Spinners, Dyers and Weavers held an exhibition, one display showed 60 different yellows. Strongest colours are usually obtained from fresh flower-heads.

Golden Rod (Solidago *species*)
There are many types of gold rod; the solidago species grow in gardens in North America and Europe. The yellow flowers, which grow in spikes, can be picked as they come into flower. They give a good strong colour at this time, but they can be dried and used later on. Leaves and stems can also be used.

Method
Simmer the flower heads. When the colour is satisfactory, strain the petals and cool the liquid. Then enter the wetted-out yarn. Bring to the boil and simmer for about ½ hour. Rinse the wool twice and dry in the shade.
Resulting colours:

Alum	— bright yellow
Chrome	— golden yellow
Iron	— olive green
Tin	— brassy yellow

Lady's bedstraw (*Galium verum*)

Pansy (Viola species)

When gardeners are clearing the pansy beds there will be a plentiful supply of pansy petals. I saw a clear green obtained from yellow pansies in a Somerset Guild exhibition in Wells Cathedral and could not wait to try them myself. However, my results were quite different. It must have been the water, or was it the soil or the weather?

Method

Boil mordanted wool and a potful of yellow pansy petals. Simmer until desired colours obtained. Rinse thoroughly and dry.
Resulting colours:

Alum   — lemon yellow
Chrome — cinnamon
Iron   — dark olive
Tin   — bright light gold
The colours were clear and strong.

Rose (Rosa species)

Red rose petals were very disappointing. Dull drab colours were obtained.

Marigold (Tagetes species)

These marigolds are also known as African marigolds or French marigolds, and they have lemon, yellow or golden flowers. They can be found in Great Britain, parts of the United States, Mexico and South America. Good strong colours are obtained from marigold heads used either fresh or dried.

Method

Simmer the flower heads. Colour will run freely and quickly from the petals. Strain the liquid, cool, then enter the clean wetted-out wool. Bring to the boil and simmer for about half an hour. Rinse the wool thoroughly and dry in the shade.
Resulting colours:

Alum   — golden yellow
Chrome — nut brown
Iron   — brown with an underglow of yellow
Tin   — bright golden orange
Cotton and nylon yarns dyed well in the same dyebath, but the colours were greenish in appearance.

Dahlia (Dahlia species)

The flowers from dahlias give excellent results when soaked in cold water with mordanted wool. In two days good strong colours are obtained from fresh or dead flower heads.
Resulting colours from orange flower heads:

Alum   — golden orange
Chrome — clear golden orange
Iron   — olive

Marigolds (*Tagetes* species)

Dahlias (*Dahlia* species)

Tin   — bright orange

Nylon yarn mordanted in alum was dyed in the same jar and became clear bright yellow.

'Solar' dyeing

In her book *How to Dye in Your Kitchen* Joan Rippengal describes how to dye without cooking. Bright clean colours can be obtained when using flowers. Large wide-mouthed glass jars are used in this method. Place alternate layers of dyestuff and mordanted wool in the jar, and almost fill it with clean, soft water. Screw the lid on loosely and stand the jar in a sunny spot. Stir the mixture every day or two. It should take from about two to nine days for the colour to be satisfactory. When emptying the jar take it outside, for the smell of decaying vegetable matter can be very unpleasant. Rinse the wool once or twice in clear water and then dry it. Coreopsis with alum mordant is especially recommended.

Joan Rippengal also suggests testing dyes in jam jars on window sills in this way and she says that the method works almost as well with unmordanted wool. In this case, add mordant to the water. If chrome mordant is used the results may be paler colours because of its sensitivity to light.

Flowers usually give the best dyes but some leaves give good results too. The latest results of my experiments were quite startling.

	Mordanted wool dyed in cold water plus washing-up liquid and petals for two days.				Mordanted wool dyed in cold water plus acetic acid and petals for two days			
Dye	Alum	Chrome	Iron	Tin	Alum	Chrome	Iron	Tin
Purple sweet peas	Deep bottle green	Blue/ green	Dark bottle green	Clear dark green	Deep indigo	Dove grey	Slate grey	Elephant grey
Red rose petals	Apple green	Biscuit	Hazel	Delicate green	Dull apple green	Beige	Mouse brown	Fawn
Fuchsia petals	Sand	Warm cream	Greyish brown	Light sand	Corn	Dull gold	Donkey brown	Golden corn

Flowers, leaves and stems

These can be used at the same time from many plants. Sometimes it is almost impossible to separate them, but it is worth experimenting with each part if possible in order to see the effect on the colour.

Agrimony (Agrimonia eupatoria)

This plant which grows to a height of 30–50 cm (12–20 in.) has little yellow flowers growing in spikes. In the olden days it was used to treat snake-bite and the flowers were put into lemonade to cure colds. It is a common plant in northern Europe and is sometimes found in eastern North America.

Method

Heat leaves and stalks slowly, then simmer for 1 hour. Strain the liquid, cool it, and add the mordanted wetted-out wool. Simmer for just long enough to obtain the desired colour. Rinse the wool well and dry.

Resulting colours:

Alum   — yellow
Chrome — gold
Iron   — khaki
Tin   — bright yellow

Like many other plants, agrimony can give slightly different shades of yellow, gold and orange according to the part of the country in which it was grown.

Agrimony (*Agrimonia eupatoria*)

Blended fleece: indigo, cochineal and weld

Cotton warps. From left to right they show: random dyeing – the
result was achieved by dipping sections of the warp into a
dye-bath, and the effect of two different threadings through the
reed using a warp which has been tie-dyed

Dyeing with orchil on wool and
on silk

Bracken (Pteridium aquilinum)

Bracken tips are easily obtained for they grow abundantly in waste places. Bracken is the most widespread of all ferns and is found in every continent except Antarctica. It grows in the tropics and in temperate regions right up to the Arctic circle. It is a pest in grassland and difficult to eradicate. The leaves have curled fronds and if these are collected from young plants a good colour can be obtained.

Method

Steep young shoots in hot water for 1½ hours. Strain and cool the liquid. Enter the clean wetted-out wool. Bring to a simmer and cook for ¾ hour. Rinse and dry.

Resulting colours:

Alum   — lemon-yellow to light green
Chrome — lime green
Iron   — dull green
Tin   — bright lemon-yellow

Dyer's Greenweed (Genista tinctoria)

This plant used to be extensively cultivated for its greenish-yellow dye, and for its value in making green when used in conjunction with indigo. It has a bushy growth and looks rather like a small broom. The leaves are very small and the flowers yellow. Flowers can be used fresh or dried, along with the leaves.

Method

Cut up the flower tops, leaves and stems, then place them in cold water and heat slowly. Simmer for one hour, then strain and cool the liquid. Enter the clean, wetted-out wool. Simmer for up to one hour or for less time if a pale colour is required. Rinse thoroughly.

Resulting colours:

Alum   — light yellow
Chrome — warm yellow
Iron   — olive green
Tin   — bright yellow

Weld or dyer's rocket (Reseda luteola)

Weld is one of my favourite dyes. There is a variety of wild mignonette (reseda lutea) which is not as sweet-scented as the garden variety. It grows

49

30–60 cm (12–24 in.) tall and is common in waste places and in ploughed fields on chalky soil. The flower stem is solid and rough and the flowers usually have six sepals and six petals. Colours obtained from this plant are weaker than those from *reseda luteola*.

Reseda luteola is taller than wild mignonette and has a hollow, unbranched or slightly branched stem. It has narrow leaves with wavy edges, which are not divided into leaflets. There are usually four sepals and four petals. It is more common than *reseda lutea*, especially in the south of England. It can be found growing around the Mediterranean and in many parts of the world. I have found it on the edge of a new by-pass in the south of England and on waste ground near a coal-mine in West Yorkshire. It grows to a height of about 1 metre (3 ft) and has long spikes of yellowish flowers. Every part of the plant except the root can be used for dyeing.

Collect the weld just before it seeds. The strongest colour is obtained when the plant is fresh, but the stems can be used any time. Let them dry by hanging them up in the shade and

Dyer's Greenweed (*Genista tinctoria*)

then tie the stalks in bundles for future use.

Weld is one of the most reliable British dye plants. It has a very long history and was highly prized by the ancient Romans. It is a particularly good dye for silk.

Method
Break the stems into small pieces or chop them up with a stainless steel knife. Steep in cold water for several hours. Decide on the way to use the dyestuff. For the brightest colour add dyestuff to the dye-bath with the required amount of water. Alternatively the dyestuff can be put in a muslin bag, or after steeping and boiling it can be strained.

Resulting colours:
Alum   — clear lemon yellow
Chrome — warm yellow
Iron   — olive greenish
Tin   — bright lemon yellow
NB A little chalk added to the dye-bath makes the colour more intense. Common salt makes the colour richer and deeper.

Chart showing the results of putting seven different samples into a weld dye-bath

	Alum	Chrome	Iron	Tin
Fleece	Clear yellow	Gold	Olive	Acid yellow
Welsh 2-ply wool	Light buttercup yellow	Gold	Brownish-olive	Clear bright yellow
Mercerized cotton yarn	Cream	Cream	Dull cream	Pale yellowish-cream
Raffia	Natural	Light gold	Deep cream	Yellowish-cream
Cotton cloth	Straw-coloured	Light biscuit	Ecru	Light cream
Silk cloth	Primrose-yellow	Slightly deeper primrose	Dull fawn	Warm yellow
Nylon yarn	Pale golden yellow	Rich golden yellow	Light khaki	Clear yellow

Leaves and stalks

Leaves and stalks tend to give greener shades of yellow. Rhubarb leaves will produce green.

Lily of the Valley (Convallaria majalis)
This is a garden flower which has white flowers with a fragrant scent. I use the leaves to obtain a dark olive green.

Method
Chop up the leaves and bring them to the boil. Cool the liquid, add the wetted-out wool which has been mordanted in iron. Alternatively, dye the wool in the liquid first, lift out the yarn, stir in iron mordant, and replace the yarn. Simmer for 15 minutes. Rinse the wool well and then dry.
Resulting colour with an iron mordant: dark olive green.

Stinging nettles (Urtica dioica)
This plant can reach a height of 1.5 m (5 ft) and grows throughout the British Isles in woods, waste places, by hedges and grassland. From June onwards it has tiny green-white flowers. When picking the leaves for dyeing it is advisable to wear gloves because the stinging hairs have a pointed single cell above a bulbous base which holds a poisonous liquid. These brittle hairs break off after piercing the skin and allow the poison to enter the wound. This causes great irritation. Nettles have other uses: they can be boiled and eaten like a vegetable; dried leaves make nettle tea, and fibres used to be spun from their stems. Stained thermos flasks and glass vases can be made clean and sparkling by rinsing them with cold water and nettle leaves.

Method
Fill a pan with nettles, bring to the boil. Cool the liquid and enter the well-wetted yarn. Bring to the boil and then simmer for half an hour. Rinse twice and dry in the shade.
Resulting colours:
Alum — pale olive green
Chrome — light olive green
Iron — dull olive green
Tin — bright olive green

Horsetail (Equisetum genus)
Horsetail is a primitive plant and can be found in ditches and damp places. It is especially useful for a clear lime green.

Method
Simmer fresh plants together with the mordanted yarn. After-bath — add one teaspoonful of copper

sulphate to dye-bath. Simmer in this mixture for ½ hour.
Resulting colours:
Tin mordant — yellow
Copper sulphate after-bath — good clear green

Skins

Skins and peel provide useful colours. Onion skins give particularly strong colours and pomegranate peel is a popular choice in some countries.

Onion skins (Allium cepa)
Onion skins make a very useful dye. The colour obtained is strong and always seems to be reliable. There are usually plenty of onion skins available — school canteens use a large amount of onions and often skins are left in the bottom of boxes in the greengrocer's. After peeling onions, the skins can be kept in a paper bag indefinitely. In Northumberland onion skins are boiled in the saucepan with eggs at Easter time and make the shells a beautiful deep golden colour.

Method
Simmer the onion skins in soft water for about ½ hour. A lovely golden liquid will soon appear. The skins can then be strained and the liquid allowed to cool. Immerse the yarn in the liquid, bring to the boil and then simmer until the desired colour is obtained.
Resulting colours:

Alum   — golden yellow
Chrome — deep gold
Iron   — khaki
Tin   — yellowish-orange

Chart showing the results of putting seven different samples into an onion dye-bath

	Alum	Chrome	Iron	Tin
Fleece	Deep gold	Golden-orange	Olive-brown	Bright golden orange
Welsh 2-ply wool	Ginger	Deeper shade of ginger	Dark brown	Bright deep orange
Mercerized cotton yarn	Light gold	Light gold	Fawn	Warm biscuit
Raffia	Dull gold	Dull gold	Burnt sienna	Clear dull orange
Cotton cloth	Golden buff	Beige	Dull fawn	Buttercup yellow
Silk cloth	Clear gold	Light gold	Olive green	Bright golden yellow
Nylon yarn	Deep gold	Brighter gold	Darker gold	Clear bright gold

Berries

Berries will supply a rich source of colouring. Now that it is easy to keep fruits in the freezer, they are available throughout the year.

Notice especially the effect on the colour when the rinsing water is acid, alkaline or neutral.

Sloe or Blackthorn (Prunus spinosa)
These trees are found growing in hedges in Europe, Asia and North America. The blue-black berries, which can be collected in autumn, are small and hard. They have such a sharp taste that they dry up the inside of the mouth when eaten. However, when used to make sloe gin the resulting drink is delicious.

Method
Use 250 g (8 oz) freshly picked fruit and 120 g (4 oz) wool.
Fruit and wool can be boiled together. Bruise the fruit well and place in a muslin bag. The water

will turn a maroon colour. Allow the wool to simmer for about 40 minutes.
Resulting colours:
Alum   — deep rose pink
Chrome — dull khaki
Iron   — purplish-pink
Tin   — brownish-purple

When rinsed in a mild soapy solution the wool mordanted in alum becomes more bluish in colour, but when rinsed in a strong detergent it turns to slate grey. An acid rinse hardly changes the colour, except that a white vinegar makes the colour a little lighter, while a brown vinegar makes it a little darker.

An acid or alkali rinse makes little difference to the resulting colour of wool mordanted in chrome, iron or tin.

Ivy (Hedera helix)
Ivy is a woody evergreen found on walls, in woods and hedges throughout the British Isles, in Asia and North America. The fruit is a black berry. February and March are the best months for picking them in Europe.

Method
Steep the ripe berries overnight. Heat them in this water and simmer for 1 hour. Remove the berries, cool the liquor and then enter the wool. Simmer for ½ hour. Sadden with iron for a greenish grey.
Resulting colours:
Alum   — yellow-green
Chrome — dull yellowish-green
Iron   — greenish-grey
Tin   — dull green
I found my colours rather pale and disappointing.

Elderberries (Sambucus nigra)
Lovely juicy purple elderberries can be found growing in the hedgerows in September. Delicious wine, tasting like port wine, is made from them, and it is used hot for curing colds. For dyeing collect the berries when they are ripe. Crush them and boil them in soft water. If stems are left on, the colour will be slightly different from that obtained with berries only.

Follow the general directions for using berries.

Resulting colours:
Alum   — purple
Chrome — slightly bluish-purple
Iron   — greyish-purple
Tin   — violet
The bark can be used for grey, and the leaves for yellowish-greens.

Blackberries (Rubus fruticosus)
There are several hundred species, and they can be found in woods and hedges throughout Britain.

Pick blackberries from the hedgerows in late summer, extract the juice and dye the wool. Young shoots can be cut and boiled to give grey.
Resulting colours:
Alum   — brownish-pink
Chrome — dull brownish-pink
Iron   — pinkish-brown
Tin   — violet
Tin mordant has a remarkable effect on the colour: it becomes a bright violet.

Sumach (Rhus species)
This tree is found in temperate and sub-tropical regions of Asia and Europe. *Rhus glabra* (smooth) and *Rhus typhina* (staghorn) are both non-poisonous varieties and can be recognized from their red berries. *Rhus radicans* and *Rhus vernix* are not recommended for dyeing as they are poisonous. Their berries are white when ripe.

Method
Soak 1 kg (2¼ lb) of ripe red berries for two hours and then dye the yarn.
Resulting colours:
Alum   — brown
Chrome — warm tan

6
Historical Dyes

Many dyes which were used hundreds of years ago have been proved to be highly successful and still give reliable, pleasing colours. Recipes have often been lost, but we have the opportunity to make discoveries for ourselves as a result of our own experiments, together with the help of clues which can sometimes be found in old books or manuscripts.

Woad (*Isatis tinctoria*)

Woad is a fascinating and tantalizing dye to use. In England woad is always associated with the Ancient Britons.

Woad grows in southern Europe, in the temperate zone. In some parts of the world it is classed as a noxious weed. Woad was grown in the British Isles in Hampshire, the Midlands and Yorkshire and in Ireland. In the eighteenth century Somerset and East Anglia became the main areas for woad cultivation. Much useful information concerning the cultivation and dyeing of woad can be obtained in the booklet *Woad in the Fens* by Norman T. Wills. He describes the old woad mills and the way woad was extracted.

The woad plant is a biennial. Its leaves are pale green, growing on an erect stem which can reach over 1 m (3 ft) in height. There is a mass of yellow flowers which turn to purple seed pods.

Woad (*Isatis tinctoria*)

A blue dye can be made from the green leaves of woad

Woad cultivation

There has been a great revival of interest in growing woad. It can easily be grown in the garden. The seed is collected in the second year. I plant mine indoors in February and transplant the seedlings in April, about 50 cm (20 in) apart. They can also be planted outside in late spring.

Woad manufacture up to 1932

In order to prepare the green leaves for dyeing, they had to go through many processes including crushing, balling, drying and crushing again, followed by couching. This drying, powdering and fermenting was a very smelly business. The last woad mills in the world, in Lincolnshire, were closed in the 1930s (Skirlbeck Mill closed after the 1932 crop).

Indigo eventually replaced woad.

Practical experiments using woad

I have spent many years trying to obtain blue from woad leaves. My first experiments, suggested by J.B. Hurry in his book *The Woad Plant and its Dye*, were only successful in producing the 'foul smell'. However, my failures were mainly due to the fact that I chose unsuitable leaves at the wrong time of year. Old leaves turning blue looked so promising; I should have used young leaves, picked before the plant flowered.

The following recipe is given by Norman T. Wills in his book *Woad in the Fens*.

1 Pick and cut up a large jarful of fresh woad leaves taken between June and October.

2 Fill the jar of leaves to the brim with almost boiling water.

3 Wait for the air bubbles to rise. Fill the jar again and put on the lid to exclude all air.

4 After 30–40 minutes the liquid will be coloured.

5 Put this liquid into jars containing one of the following strong alkalis: ammonia, soda, caustic potash or wood ash.

6 Shake each jar thoroughly and the liquid becomes dark green.

7 Drop clean wool into the liquid. This will become blue on exposure to the air.

8 Repeated dippings will give darker shades.

This method is not fast to soap.

The following recipe is recommended by Seonaid Robertson in her book *Dyes from Plants* (© Van Nostrand Reinhold Company 1973)

1 Pack 250 g (8 oz) of young fresh leaves into a jar and press them down tightly.

2 Pour over water which has been heated to just under boiling point. Press down leaves so that no air remains when the top is screwed on.

3 Keep this at about 40°–60°C for 6–12 hours.

4 Allow to cool until small bubbles rise.

5 Open the jar and stir in 6 g ($\frac{1}{5}$ oz) lime (calcium oxide) or a few tablespoons of ammonia.

55

6 The yellowish liquid will begin to turn greenish-yellow.

7 Enter clean, wetted wool.

8 Steep the wool for one hour, then lift it out with a glass rod. It will turn blue in contact with the air.

Darker colours will be obtained if dippings are repeated.

I cannot claim success with this method. My best blues have been obtained by using ammonia or calcium hydroxide (slaked lime) with sodium dithionite. The fresh green leaves, taken from the plant before it flowers, have to be broken up and placed in boiling water. I then boil them for about two minutes, strain them and work with the brownish-green liquid. The alkali, either lime or ammonia, is added to the liquid when it has cooled. Use enough alkali to turn the liquid bright yellowish-green. When lime is added blue bubbles quickly appear on the surface. After this I heat the liquid to about 85°C and add a salt-spoonful of sodium dithionite for every litre (1¾ pints) of liquid. Yarn can now be dyed. It will appear greenish-yellow in the dye-bath but when exposed to the air it will turn blue. The dyeing is followed by an acid rinse, a soapy rinse and lastly a rinse of clear water.

When samples of cotton, nylon, wool and an acrylic/nylon mixture were dyed with young woad leaves each yarn dyed well, with cotton giving the lightest blue. However, woad crops vary and much patience may be needed before a good colour is obtained. It is worth it in the end.

Colours resulting from experiments

	Method	Colour of yarn
Young woad leaves (first year)	Ammonia and sodium dithionite	Pale to dark blue
Woad leaves in Second year	Ammonia and sodium dithionite	No colour
Yellow woad flowers	Boiled in soft water	Fawn
Woad stems after flowering	Boiled in soft water	Very pale greyish-blue when lime was added to the water

Indigo *(Indigofera tinctoria)*

Indigo has been one of the most important and popular dyes from ancient and medieval times until today. It is obtained from the leaves of the *indigofera tinctoria*, a plant which grows in Asia, Africa, the East Indies, the Philippines and America. It has a romantic history. For more than 5,000 years this product, which was originally obtained from the sap of certain leguminous plants, has been a most important dye-stuff. Woad and indigo were the main sources of blue dye. At first, indigo was viewed with great suspicion and woad growers did everything in their power to stop indigo being used. Many fears and superstitions were fostered by the woad cultivators, for they were afraid of the competition which indigo would bring. Repressive laws were passed in England, France and Germany prohibiting the importation of indigo. It was called 'devil's food', and a pernicious drug; a number of dangerous properties were attributed to it. However, in the end indigo replaced the home-grown woad, and the cultivation and extraction of indigo became an important Indian industry. In the second half of the nineteenth century the world's consumption of indigo was estimated at five million kilogrammes (5,000 tons) but at the end of the century a dramatic change came about as the result of a German scientist's discovery. In 1866 Professor Adolph von Baeyer began his researches into the dyestuff and found out the precise chemical structure of the indigo molecule. This revolutionized the method of manufacture and led to the development of artificial dyestuffs sharing the valuable properties of indigo. A rainbow of colours followed this great breakthrough.

The indigo molecule consists of a complex assembly of carbon, hydrogen, nitrogen and oxygen atoms connecting two benzene rings. By 1907 the synthetic manufacture of indigo was a firmly established German industry and the consumption of natural indigo steadily decreased. A large factory was built in England at Ellesmere Port on the river Mersey in 1908 to supply requirements of the British market. The Ellesmere Port factory has produced indigo continuously from 1916 onwards and this famous dyestuff appears to increase in popularity yearly.

What is it about indigo that makes it so popular? It possesses a number of properties which have not all been incorporated in any other single dyestuff. These properties include its attractive shade, the ability to build up heavy navy shades by repeated dippings, the ability to dye cotton from a cold dyebath and good general fastness properties. The outstanding characteristic that makes indigo so special is its property of maintaining its tone after repeated severe washings and exposure to light. Although indigo-dyed fabric can lose its depth of colour, the tone is still pleasing. The fashion world calls it 'that been-in-the-sun look'.

Indigo dyeing thrives as a local cottage industry in villages throughout West Africa and the Far East.

The indigo dyeing method used in the bazaar cloth dyeing trade is wholly manual and in many cases it has remained unchanged for centuries.

Often holes in the ground are used for the dyebath and the liquor is heated over open fires. Open air is used for oxidization and drying. Materials are readily available, many of them occurring naturally, and include natural fermentation products such as wood ashes which act as the reducing and alkali-solubilizing agents.

I have read in an *Organic News* supplement that indigo dye-bath ingredients might still be measured out with equipment that happens to come readily to hand. Ingredients lists have been known to take this form:

1 kerosene tin of water
½ cigarette tin lid of salt
2 cigarette tin lids each of caustic soda flake, hydrosulphite and carpenter's glue
½ paint tin lid of indigo 60 per cent grains

Many recipes are available for dyeing with indigo, but I use a very simple one.

The Merheim Method

Germain Merheim was a research chemist who worked out a simple method for dyeing vat colours. He called it his 'jam jar and teaspoon' method. The interesting thing is that vat dyestuffs, which are extremely fast colours but quite difficult to apply, need similar treatment to indigo and woad. These dyestuffs are not soluble in water so the insoluble dyestuff has to be reduced by means of caustic soda and sodium dithionite to form a soluble leuco compound which has direct affinity for fibres. The original dyestuff is produced on the fibre after dyeing, by air oxidization.

Recipe for indigo

3 kg (7 lb) stone jam jar
Water at 50°C (hot to the hand)
120 g (4 oz) cotton which should have been well boiled
1 teaspoon sodium dithionite (formerly called sodium hydrosulphite)
1 teaspoon sodium hydroxide
1–3 teaspoons indigo powder

1   Fill the stone jam jar or similar container one-third full of water at 50°C.

2   Dissolve 1 teaspoonful of sodium hydroxide in warm water and 1 teaspoonful of sodium dithionite in warm water. Add these carefully to the water in the jam jar.

3   Add to this liquid 1–3 teaspoonfuls of indigo powder. The colour will change to a greenish yellow. Try to avoid getting air into this mixture. If the jam jar is held between the hands and gently shaken round the indigo will become dissolved in this liquor.

NB Oxygen is removed from indigo with sodium dithionite and is changed into indigo white which will dissolve in an alkali — in this case sodium hydroxide.

4 After ten minutes fill the jam jar with water at 50°C until it is two-thirds full.

5 Give the jar another gentle shake.

6 Enter well-boiled and wetted-out cotton — try to avoid making bubbles.

7 Work the skeins carefully in the dye liquor.

8 Leave for five minutes.

Repeat 7 and 8.

9 Lift the skeins out of the jar with a glass rod and let them drain.

10 Hang them in the air for 20–30 minutes. As if by magic the skeins change colour. At first they appear to be greenish yellow, then green and finally a permanent blue. De-oxidized indigo is yellow; as it takes oxygen from the air it becomes blue.

11 Rinse twice in warm water to remove caustic soda.

12 Rinse once in acid water (1 tablespoonful of acetic acid to a small bucket) to neutralize remaining soda.

13 Rinse again in warm acid-free water to remove all acid.

14 Wash well in very hot soapy water (Germain used boiling water) to get rid of any loose dye.

15 Rinse thoroughly and dry.

Build up a shade by dipping the skeins in the liquid several times but remember to let the yarn oxidize before each dipping. The liquid will be getting colder, but it will still dye the cotton until the colour has been exhausted.

This recipe can be used on wool but always be very careful when measuring the sodium hydroxide.

A range of colours can be produced which will be very useful when top-dyeing.

Indigo-dyed cotton fades but wool dyed with indigo shows little evidence of fading.

Logwood *(Haematoxylon campechianum)*

Logwood is also known as Campeachy wood because it was discovered by the Spaniards on the Bay of Campeachy in Mexico. The tree is fairly large.

Freshly cut wood is colourless until it is exposed to oxidization by air, then the outside becomes a dark reddish-brown. Logwood was used in Spain for dyeing early in the sixteenth century but was apparently not used in England until the reign of Elizabeth I. In 1580 an Act of Parliament forbade the use of logwood — it was thought to be a fugitive colour. It does rub off if the dyed yarn is not thoroughly rinsed.

Recipe for logwood
120 g (4 oz) wool
10–30 g ($\frac{1}{3}$–1 oz) logwood chips (amount varies according to shade required)
4.5 litres (1 gallon) soft water

Logwood can be used in the same way as weld. On the whole I prefer to tie the chips in a muslin bag, for the little pieces of wood cling to the wool. Resulting colours:

Alum — violet and purplish grey

Chrome — the bluest shade is obtained from chrome

Iron — dark grey to black

Tin — purple

Madder *(Rubia tinctorum)*

There are about 35 species of madder plants. They vary in height from 1 to 3 metres (3–9 feet). This dye plant has been known from ancient times; there is evidence of madder-dyed cloth in Egyptian pre-dynastic tombs. The roots contain the valuable dye pigment which is obtained from between the rind and the hard central core. Old roots were considered to be richer in pigments than younger roots. In Europe the plants were left in the soil for 24 to 30 months. Madder plant roots are long and about as thick as a lead pencil.

After the roots are dug up they are thoroughly washed in pure water, allowed to dry and then ground into powder.

In the first dye trade document written in Greek, there is a record of trade in this root between India and Asia Minor. After the collapse of the Roman Empire in the fourth century AD and for almost eight centuries we know little of madder being

Opposite Madder *(Rubia tinctorum)*

grown in Europe. The dye trade moved back to the Orient, and Baghdad became the most important centre of the dye trade. In the eighth century madder plants were cultivated again. From the tenth century it was grown in Holland, and the Dutch became the most advanced madder growers in the world. A large amount of imported and local madder used in England passed through Norwich. This city became the most important madder distribution point. A local thoroughfare is still called Madder Street and there is the Madder Market Theatre.

Madder is a challenging dyestuff to use. Fawn and red both seem to be present in madder. Bright red was dyed by a long process in the Levant: this was known as Turkey red. The process of dyeing was a very long one — it is said that there were as many as 14 operations before the brilliant, lustrous, durable colour was obtained.

Recipe for madder

Before dyeing, make sure the wool has been washed well in order to get rid of surplus mordant. Use hard water and bring it to the boil slowly. If madder is boiled the colour becomes a brownish red. Madder put into muslin also appears to bring out brownish shades. The clearest vermilion, pink or red colours are obtained in hard water with the madder loose in the dye-bath as suggested in Method 1.

120 g (4 oz) wool
60 g (2 oz) madder for full shade
20 g (¾ oz) madder for pale shade
4.5 litres (1 gallon) hard water

Method 1

1 Warm the hard water to 30°C.

2 Add madder loose.

3 Enter well-wetted mordanted wool.

4 Raise the temperature very slowly to 100°C. Take 1–1½ hours over this.

5 Reduce the temperature at once to 90°C so that the colour does not turn brownish-yellow.

6 Dye the wool for about ½ hour. Move it round gently from time to time.

7 When the desired colour has been obtained, allow the wool to cool in the liquid.

8 Rinse twice in warm, clear water.

9 Rinse in soapy water (40°C).

10 Rinse in clear water, squeeze, shake skeins and dry them out of the sun.

Resulting colours:

Alum   — vermilion, rusty red

Chrome — purplish-red

Iron   — brown

Tin   — bright orange

Method 2

Instead of putting loose madder in the bath, place it in a muslin bag. Take a little longer over raising the temperature and simmering the liquid. The yarn will require working a little more in order to make sure the dyeing is level. The advantage of this method is that there will be no loose particles of madder in the wool but yellower shades will probably be produced.

Method 3

Add loose madder to the dye-bath and after steeping for a few hours raise the temperature to 90°C. Keep it at this temperature for ½ hour. Then strain the liquid after it has cooled. Add this liquid to the dye-bath and continue as from Method 1 No. 3. The wool is yellowed and dull.

Preparation of madder roots

If you grow your own roots, they should be two or three years old before being dug up. Scrub them thoroughly before drying. It is thought that Eastern

madder produced brighter colours because the roots were dried in the sunshine.

This dyestuff will not be as strong as a commercial madder which can be obtained from suppliers, so use at least three times the quantity given in the recipe.

Alizarin is the chemical name of the important colouring matter found in the madder root. In 1868 alizarin was made synthetically from anthracene derived from coal tar. The growing of madder declined after that date.

Kermes *(coccus ilicis)*

Kermes insects supplied the scarlet dyestuff which was used throughout ancient and medieval times. These insects were found on the leaves of the ilex oak trees which grow in the south of Europe. They were harvested before dawn by women carrying lanterns and picking the insects from the leaves with finger nails which were kept long for this purpose. During the Renaissance, Venice was the principal trade centre of kermes dyeing and *Ecarlate de Venise* was very famous. Many reds in Gothic tapestries were produced with kermes and they were considered more permanent than later tapestries which were dyed with cochineal.

Dyeing with kermes became known as 'grain' or 'ingrain' dyeing. In *Twelfth Night*, Shakespeare uses the phrase ''Tis ingrain, Sir! 'twill endure wind and weather'.

With the discovery of America kermes insects had a competitor in the cochineal insect. A very interesting study entitled *The Grain Tree* has been published by the Society of Dyers and Colourists. The following recipe found in a book written in 1750 is taken from the Society's study.

To make scarlet of grain

The [worsted] yarns are washed for 30 minutes at the boil in a bath containing 1½ pints of bran (in a linen bag), for every pound weight of wool (weighed dry), and the 'necessary quantity' of water.

[It is usual to hang the hanks of yarn from smooth sticks, supported by the upper edges of the vessel. Use one pound of yarn to each stick (the vessel deep enough for the hanks to hang freely). A second stick is used to turn the hanks, so that all parts receive equal treatment].

Next, after wringing-out the hanks, they are treated at the boil for two hours in a fresh bath containing 20 per cent of Roman Alum and 10 per cent of 'red tartar', (reckoned on the dry-weight of the wool), and acidulated with a pint of 'sour bran-water' for each gallon of water. (The hanks should be turned continually). After draining, the hanks are wrapped in a clean linen cloth, previously wetted-out in the Alum-bath, and they are then stored in a cool place for five or six days, before dyeing them.

Finally, the hanks are dyed in a fresh bath of clean soft water. 12 oz [340 g] of powdered or crushed Kermes grains are added to the bath for each 1 lb [454 g] (dry weight) of wool. The dye is added when the water is tepid and the hanks are put in when it approaches the boil and are then turned quickly. (The hanks should still be evenly moist, if they have developed dry-spots they must be wet out thoroughly in warm water and wrung-out evenly before dyeing). The freshly prepared dye-bath often has a slight blackish scum on the surface, and this is removed by throwing in a handful of clean wool waste for a few moments, before putting in the yarn. Dyeing should continue at the boil for the time required to obtain 'an even dyeing of the depth desired'.

The partially exhausted bath might be used for a batch of pink or to redden an orange or a violet or a 'murray', previously coloured with other dyes.

Cochineal (coccus cacti)

The cochineal insect was brought to Europe by the Spanish in the early sixteenth century after the discovery of America. The Aztecs had been using cochineal dye for centuries. Cochineal insects take three months to mature so a crop of about 90 kg (14 stone) per acre was usually collected during May, July and October. When the rainy season came branches of cactus plants which were loaded with young insects were cut off and taken indoors to prevent the insects being destroyed by stormy weather.

Cochineal insects were brushed from cactus leaves into bags or wooden bowls. They were killed by being put into boiling water, in heated ovens or by exposure to the hot sun. About 50,000 are required to weigh 1 kg (2¼ lb) and it has been estimated that about 70,000 dried insects are required to produce 500 g ($1\frac{1}{8}$ lb) of cochineal dye.

The Spaniards had a monopoly in the sale of cochineal. They forbade the export of live cochineal insects and tried to keep the origin of the dyestuff a secret. Not until 1643 was a dye-house for scarlet established in England. Until about 1725 it was generally believed that cochineal was the seed of an American tropical plant.

Recipe for cochineal

120 g (4 oz) clean wetted-out wool mordanted in alum
7–15 g (¼–½ oz) cochineal (depending on shade required)
4.5 litres (1 gallon) soft water
1 teaspoon common salt

1 Steep cochineal and salt overnight. Then strain the liquid and add it to the dye-bath. This will prevent the little pieces of cochineal, like grit, from becoming mixed up with the wool.

2 Heat water in dye-bath to 30°C.

3 Enter the yarn. Raise to the boil, taking 1 hour. Then simmer for 1 hour. When the liquid is cool rinse the wool in warm water, squeeze and dry.

To obtain a brighter red, lift the yarn out of the dye-bath ½ hour before completing the dyeing and add 2 g ($\frac{1}{16}$ oz) tin crystals which must be dissolved in warm water first. Return the yarn and simmer for another ½ hour. After dyeing rinse the yarn well in soapy water and then in clear water before drying.

Scarlet with tin mordant

This is a very popular colour; it is very bright and clear. British Guardsmen's uniform used to be dyed with cochineal, and one factory in the West Country still used it until 1957.

Recipe for cochineal

120 g (4 oz) clean wetted-out wool
3 g ($\frac{1}{10}$ oz) tin crystals
7 g (¼ oz) cream of tartar
7–15g (¼–½ oz) cochineal

1 Dissolve tin crystals in a small pot of warm water, and cream of tartar in a pot of hot water.

2 Prepare the dye by covering the cochineal with water and adding the mordant and cream of tartar. Boil for 5 minutes.

3 Prepare the dye-bath with warm water and add the dyestuff and mordant which have just been boiled. Stir well.

4 Enter the yarn and work for 5 minutes.

5 Take 45 minutes to raise the temperature to 95°C. Work yarn gently.

6 Continue dyeing for up to 1 hour, depending on depth of colour required.

7 Remove from heat and allow to cool. Then rinse in warm water followed by an acid rinse (water and acetic acid), then a soapy rinse. Lastly rinse in clear water and dry.

Resulting colours when using four mordants:

Alum   — clear red to pink

Chrome — purplish-red

Iron   — greyish-violet

Tin   — scarlet

Fustic *(Chlorophora tinctoria)*

Old fustic is the golden yellow wood of a large tree called *chlorophora tinctoria* which grows wild in the West Indies and tropical America. It was first brought to Europe by the Spaniards at the beginning of the sixteenth century. Fustic is sold in the form of wooden chips.

Recipe for Fustic

120 g (4 oz) wool
25 g ($\frac{4}{5}$ oz) fustic chips
Soft water

Tie the chips in a muslin bag to prevent them getting tangled in the wool. Soak the chips overnight and then use this liquid in the dye-bath. Proceed as for other dye woods.

Resulting colours:

Alum   — clear yellow

Chrome — golden yellow

Iron   — olive greenish-yellow

Tin   — bright yellow

Old fustic and young fustic

There may be confusion over these names. Young fustic (*rhus cotinus* or Venice sumach) is a shrub growing in Italy and the south of France. The root and stem are used for dyeing a golden yellow to orange on wool mordanted with tin. The colour is fugitive.

Old fustic was given this name by the English; the French call it *bois jaune*. It is incorrect to think of old fustic and young fustic as the same tree, only differing in age.

Safflower *(Carthamus tinctorius)*

The safflower plant, not to be confused with saffron (*crocus sativus*) is an annual plant, first cultivated in Spain, Egypt and the Levant. It grows to 1 m (3 feet) in height. The dye content consists of a water-soluble yellow and a water-insoluble red component. This dye is found in the floret heads which are about 2.5 cm (1 in.) diameter. The florets are carefully picked by hand, thoroughly dried in the sun or first washed to remove the fugitive yellow dye, thus leaving the insoluble red dye. It is a useful dye because orange, red and shades of pink can be obtained depending on the use of acids or alkalis. Chinese dyers are said to have obtained rose, scarlet, purple and violet shades on silk and the Egyptians used it on linen to obtain brilliant scarlet.

Safflower is recommended for cotton dyeing. According to Hummel (*The Dyeing of Textile Fabrics*) the cotton is worked for some time in a cold carbonate of soda solution of the colouring matter, removed from the bath, and the solution is slightly acidified with sulphuric acid or tartaric acid. The cotton is put into the bath again and the real dyeing only happens in the acid bath. The dyed cotton is afterwards rinsed in slightly acidified water.

Saffron *(crocus sativus)*

Saffron was the principal yellow dyestuff used by the Greeks and Romans. It was obtained from the pistils of the *crocus sativus* which flowers in September or October. Medieval cooks and physicians as well as dyers used the fine powder of the dried crocus. An early figure subject in fresco-painting is

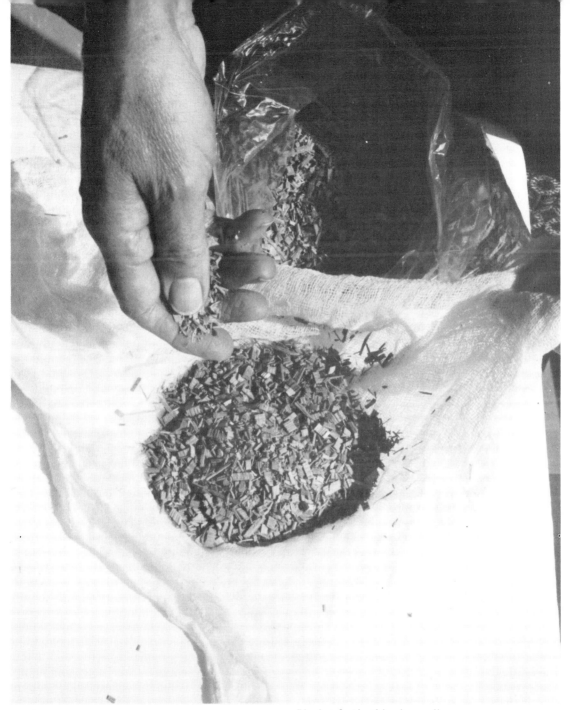

Placing fustic chips in muslin

the saffron gatherer of Knossos. As more than 4,000 dried stigmata were required to produce 30 g (1 oz) of dyestuff, other yellow dyestuffs were eventually used. Basle adopted the saffron blossom as part of its coat of arms and for ten years after AD 1420 saffron was profitably grown there. It is said that saffron was brought to England in the reign of Edward III by a pilgrim who hid two saffron corms in his staff. Saffron Walden, in Essex, gets its name from saffron and the crocus is included in its coat of arms. Growers of saffron were called 'crokers'. Saffron can be bought from chemists' shops, but it is expensive. Market stalls in Heraklion in Crete have a plentiful supply. Saffron is also exported from Spain.

Recipe for saffron

1 Gently boil 30 g (1 oz) of dried saffron for ½ hour.

2 Strain the liquid into the dye-bath.

3 Immerse mordanted, wetted wool or silk in lukewarm dye-bath.

4 Simmer wool gently. If dyeing silk dye it at a lower temperature (70°C).

5 Rinse carefully and dry in the shade.

Resulting colours:

Alum   – warm yellow

Chrome – golden yellow

Iron   – dull brownish-yellow

Tin   – bright yellow

Quercitron – Black Oak *(Quercus velutina* formerly known as *Quercus tinctoria)*

The black oak has downy twigs and hairy buds with dark green, shiny leaves which are pale and downy below. The tree is common in the United States but does not grow in Britain.

It is from the bark of this tree that a very popular dye was obtained in the eighteenth century. Edward Bancroft in his book *Experimental Researches Concerning the Philosophy of Permanent Colours* (1794) said he was delighted with this dye and described its uses with great affection. It is interesting to note that the use and application of *quercus tinctoria* for dyeing, calico printing, etc. was exclusively vested in him for a number of years by an Act of Parliament.

These are his reasons for promoting quercitron:

1 It was much cheaper than other yellow dyes because less is required in the dye-bath.

2 Weld, a very popular dye, took up much more land, and it depended on the weather to produce good crops.

3 A large quantity of weld was required and would be more difficult to transport than the bark.

4 The dye ran quickly from the bark so when dyeing less labour and less heat would be needed.

5 It did not fade like young fustic.

Quercitron is available in extract form, but if stripping the bark yourself, look for the middle coat. The bark seems to consist of three parts or coats: the external coat, blackish in colour; the middle or cellular coat, which holds the colour, and the interior part.

In the external coat the yellow colouring is less pure and is inclined towards brown. It should be separated from the rest if a clear yellow is required. The middle coat is the best part to use and can be bought in powder form. The powder is made by drying the bark.

Bancroft goes into great detail concerning the use of quercitron. While you may not wish to make as many experiments with this dye, it could be useful to consider his hints, for they may be helpful in other experiments.

Hints from Bancroft

1 To get lemon add a trace of indigo or vinegar.

2 If iron and chalk are used the colour becomes chocolate brown, but with this recipe great care is needed to get an even colour.

3 Sulphate of iron and sulphate of manganese in small quantities produce a drab colour. With the addition of chalk the colour became cinnamon.

4 Cochineal with quercitron makes a more beautiful orange than madder.

5 If a small amount of quercitron is added to the cochineal dye-bath the colour looks similar to a cochineal-only dye in daylight, but in candlelight the shades look fuller.

6 Many variations can be made by increasing or diminishing the amounts of bark used with cochineal.

7 An alkali solution brings out a yellowish brown colour, while an acid solution makes the colour lighter.

8 Vary the times of putting in mordants and vary the amounts, always making sure that the

correct weight is not exceeded.

9   The unequalled lustre and brightness of quercitron yellows will make a good green compared with those which result from 'the dull muddy yellow of old fustic' — and it will cost less.

Extract of quercitron bark is called flavine and is available from suppliers. Flavine is much stronger than quercitron bark and, as it is free from tannin, its colours are brighter.

Cutch *(catechu)*

Cutch is obtained from the wood of various acacia trees. Bombay catechu is considered particularly good for dyeing; it has been used as a brown dye in India for over 2,000 years. Cutch wood is gathered when the acacia trees are green and full of sap. The bark is stripped off, then the timber is chopped into sections and boiled in water. The extract solidifies as it cools and it is formed into dark brown blocks.

Cutch is used chiefly on cotton, but it also gives a rich brown on wool and silk. It is soluble in water.

Commercially cutch was found to be a useful dye because of its good fastness properties in relation to water, washing and light. It was good for awnings, sails and nets.

Cotton material was steeped in a dye-bath of soft water with cutch and copper sulphate. It was wrung out, left to stand for several hours and then worked in a bath of bichromate of potash.

Recipe for cutch
For light grey
120 g (4 oz) clean wetted-out cotton
5 g ($\frac{1}{6}$ oz) cutch extract
4 g ($\frac{1}{7}$ oz) iron

For brown
20 g (¾ oz) cutch and mordant in iron or chrome

1   Boil cotton in cutch for ½ hour.

2   Sadden with iron mordant.

3   Wash thoroughly.

Summary of ways to obtain different shades within each dye

1   Use different mordants, which can be added at various stages in dyeing.

2   Vary the strengths of the liquor in the dye-bath.

3   Use acid, alkaline or neutral water in the dye-bath.

4   Leave the yarn in for differing lengths of time.

5   Use different kinds of pans, e.g. iron, copper, brass.

6   Heat at different speeds.

7   Rinse in various temperatures.

8   Rinse in acid, alkaline, neutral or all three types of water.

9   Change the recipes.

10   Use the same plants at different times of the year.

11   Use plants after different weather conditions, e.g. very wet, very hot and dry.

12   Use plants from different habitats.

13   Use various types of material.

14   Select material which had been prepared and treated in different ways before dyeing.

There is plenty of scope for experimenting — perhaps a pinch of this or that ingredient will make all the difference.

7
Mixing Colours

Attractive colours can be obtained by mixing dye-stuffs in the same dye-bath. There is almost always colour left in the bath after the first dyeing has taken place. This colour can be used with successive dyeings until it is completely exhausted. For example, from one dye-bath of orchil ten skeins were dyed; the first one was deep magenta-red and the last a delicate pinkish lilac. The liquor can be added to other dye-baths in order to change the shades. More than one dye can be mixed in the same bath. There is plenty of scope for experiment and individual taste. Different dyestuffs can be boiled separately and mixed in various proportions or they can be boiled together. Remember that colours can again be altered by the addition of a small amount of mordant after dyeing, either blooming or saddening by adding tin or iron.

Logwood chips

Logwood chips are very useful in helping to produce a variety of colours ranging from different types of black through to violet, lavender, grey, purple and dull greens. When choosing a mordant select chrome for the bluest tones and tin for purple. Very thorough rinsing is necessary after using logwood chips.

Dull black
Mordant with chrome. Place in the same dye-bath 30 g (1 oz) logwood chips and 6 g ($\frac{1}{5}$ oz) fustic chips. The black will be dense and dull.

Greenish-black
The black will appear greenish if more fustic is added to the dye-bath. Try experimenting with other mordants; alum, for example, will bring out the green shades.

Lavender
Mordant with chrome. Make up a dye-bath with twice as much madder as logwood. Look at the resulting colour and judge the proportions of madder to logwood when making other experiments. Rinse the wool very thoroughly and dry it in the shade in order to get the true colour result. Logwood rubs off if it is not well rinsed; I have often seen people with purple hands when they have made a warp from threads dyed in logwood, indicating that the rinsing was hurried and incomplete.

Dark red-purple
Mordant with alum and cream of tartar. Make up a dye-bath with twice as much logwood as madder. Enter the wool and simmer until the required colour is obtained.

NB Logwood chips produce a really strong colour and the dye-bath can go on being used for a large number of hanks. The deep purples eventually become a glowing mauve and then a pale delicate lavender. These colours blend together well when carding. The dark, heavy colours, like a sky before an approaching thunderstorm, are very useful for backgrounds as they enrich the colours which are used with them.

Madder

Madder likes hard water, and to prevent the colour turning brownish-yellow, raise the temperature gradually and avoid boiling.

Purplish-red

Mordant with alum. Dye with madder and add a small amount of logwood.

Brown

Mordant with iron. Add a small amount of fustic to the madder dye-bath.

Reddish-brown

Mordant with chrome. Wash well and dye with madder plus fustic and logwood in various proportions, e.g. half as much fustic as madder and a very small amount of logwood; or, equal quantities of madder and logwood plus a very small amount of fustic.

Madder can be added to the yellow dyes, particularly fustic and weld. By varying the amount, colours will range from pale old gold to maize, orange and tan. The brightness of the colours could be emphasized by using a tin mordant or by removing the wool from the dye-bath 20 minutes before concluding the dyeing and adding a small amount of tin crystals.

Cochineal

To make a rose red, mordant with alum. Mix a dye-bath with equal quantities of madder and cochineal. Twenty minutes before the end of dyeing, remove the wool and stir in a small amount of tin crystals. Replace the wool. When the colour is satisfactory, remove the wool and rinse well.

Fustic

Old gold

Mordant with chrome. Wash and then dye in fustic to which has been added a small amount of madder.

Greenish-yellow

Mordant with chrome. Wash wool and dye it in a small amount of fustic with three times that amount of logwood chips.

Take care not to leave the wool at a high simmer for too long as the yellow can become brownish and dull.

Tan

Mordant with chrome. Make a dye-bath consisting of equal quantities of fustic and madder plus a very small amount of logwood.

Greenish-black

Mordant with chrome. Dye with equal quantities of fustic, logwood and a small amount of madder. It can be saddened with iron.

Exhausting the dye-bath

Some colours automatically blend together well when taken from the dye-bath at intervals, and they make attractive colour schemes. I think of them as 'safe' colour schemes; for example, indigo looks very pleasing when changing from deep blue to sky blue, and walnut can safely be used ranging from its deep warm brown to palest fawn. But take care with cochineal. In a scarlet dye-bath the colour can go on being exhausted until it changes from bright scarlet to the palest pink. The resulting shades can be quite tricky to use together — they are not automatically 'safe' and require careful handling. But this takes us back to the problem of how to use colour, and everyone has his or her own opinion about 'good colour'.

Top dyeing

Top dyeing or over-dyeing describes the method of dyeing one colour over another. It may be that the first colour was unsatisfactory, or it needed to be changed completely. Perhaps a colour such as bright green which is unobtainable from one source is required.

If two dyeing processes are involved, it is advisable to start with the weaker or lighter colour. A dark strong colour will not so easily be influenced by a lighter colour dyed over it. As a rule it is much more satisfactory to build a colour up; it is easier to make several dips because then one can watch the shade develop. The second dyeing will not take very long if the colour is a strong one.

While the first dyeing is taking place, prepare the second dye-bath so that the whole process can be completed straightaway. The yarn, after being rinsed and squeezed from its first colour, will be evenly damp and ready for the second dye-bath. If it is impossible to complete the dyeing, keep the yarn damp in a towel and try to use it soon. If it gets dry, remember that a thorough wetting-out is necessary for level dyeing. If you only want half the skein top-dyed make one half wet and dip it into the dye.

Always keep plenty of samples handy. Never throw dye liquor away, but exhaust it by putting in odd skeins, fleece or rags. If short of time store the liquor in the fridge (well-labelled) until it can be used. As indigo is often used for top-dyeing, a pale blue from an almost exhausted indigo vat is useful to make delicate greens or mauves. The indigo vat can be used cold.

Tie-dyeing is described on page 82.

Suggested recipes

Reddish-black Dye with indigo first followed by a cochineal dye-bath.

Blue-black Dye with sumach to get grey, then use indigo.

Red-black After using sumach and indigo, dye with cochineal.

Yellow-black Dye with a strong yellow, such as onion skins or fustic. Follow this with sumach and lastly use indigo.

Flat black Dye deep brown with walnut and then dye in indigo, followed by cochineal.

Purple Logwood on a tin mordant makes purple, but a plum or violet range can be obtained by using a chrome or iron mordant first with cochineal. Then dye in indigo.

Flame Dye a clear yellow first with fustic or onion skins on a chrome mordant and then use madder.

Green

Deep green is difficult to obtain. I have used horse-tail, rhubarb leaves, lily of the valley and stinging nettles for the one dye-bath method, but apart from horse tail the colours are rather sombre. This is only my experience: I have seen good clear greens in other people's collections. Usually green has to be dyed in two stages, using blue plus yellow. As yellow has a tendency to fade, the green often appears blue after a number of years. The balance of colour schemes on old tapestries has often been

destroyed because the leaves and grass appear blue where the yellow has faded out.

Every dyer has a favourite yellow. It will affect the green depending on whether it is lemon, golden yellow or dull yellow. Choice of dyestuff and mordant is very important.

There is some question about whether to dye blue or yellow first. Those in favour of dyeing blue first feel that the mordanting which follows could help make the blue clear, whilst if yellow is dyed first the shade of green can be judged better during the indigo dips. There are no definite rules on the correct procedure.

8
Dyeing Cotton, Linen and Other Fibres

It is much more difficult to dye cotton and linen than wool with natural dyestuffs. The results are often pale and disappointing.

As with all dyeing, thorough preparation of the fibres is very important. They must be scoured, bleached, soured and mordanted if the colour is to be bright and clear. On the other hand, if a clear colour is not required, some of the preliminary stages can be left out. Whether the preparation is mild or severe depends on the effect desired.

Cotton

Is the cotton natural coloured, cream or light brown? Has it already been bleached? Is it plain or mercerized? Mercerized cotton has a lustre which will have been acquired during the mercerization process and the dye will take well.

The easiest way to dye cotton is to start with bleached, mercerized skeins, as all the preliminary stages will have been already carried out. For the dyer who wishes to start with unbleached cotton the following processes are necessary:

1 Thorough scouring

2 Bleaching

3 Souring

4 Mordanting

5 Dyeing

In countries where cotton was dyed with natural dyestuffs, madder, cutch, indigo, turmeric and fustic were among the most popular. Madder was used to produce Turkey red, but this was a very long process and is unlikely to be used by dyers today. Cutch, a very good cotton dye, produced shades of brown, grey and black. Indigo was used for shades of blue ranging from pale blue to navy.

Yellow, the colour most likely to fade, was obtained from turmeric, fustic and flavine. Green which was dyed with a mixture of yellow and blue would also have been likely to fade.

Scouring
Cotton is scoured in order to remove natural wax and other impurities.

Method
1 Boil the yarn in clean soft water for 1 hour.

2 Rinse the cotton.

3 Boil the yarn for 1–1½ hours in 4.5 litres (1 gallon) of soapy water to which has been added 7.5 g (¼ oz) of washing soda.

4 Rinse thoroughly.

Bleaching
If a clear, light colour is required after dyeing, bleaching is essential.

There are a number of household bleaches on the market which would be suitable. Follow the instructions given by the manufacturer and make up a bleaching bath using a stainless steel, galvanised or earthenware vessel. Use water in the usual ratio of 1 : 30 (litres : grams), so 4 litres (7 pints) of water will be satisfactory for 120 g (4 oz) of cotton.

1 Enter the wetted-out skeins for 2–3 hours. Turn them occasionally with a glass rod or a clean, smooth wooden rod, making sure that the liquid penetrates the fibres evenly.

2 Remove yarns from bleach, squeeze them and expose to the air for a few hours.

This process can be repeated until the yarn is white enough for dyeing, then rinse very thoroughly.

Souring

This is the next stage after scouring and bleaching. It helps to give a clearer white and to remove any metallic compounds which may cause trouble later by preventing the dye from being level.

Recipe

10 g ($\frac{1}{3}$ oz) tannic acid for full shades
3 g ($\frac{1}{10}$ oz) tannic acid for paler shades

1 Dissolve the tannic acid in a little hot water.

2 Prepare the bath with 4.5 litres (1 gallon) of cold water.

3 Add acid and enter cotton.

4 Raise the heat to 60°C and while doing so work the cotton.

5 Turn off the heat and allow yarn to steep for several hours.

Rinse thoroughly in order to remove all traces of acid and then prepare to mordant the cotton.

Mordanting

There are many ways of mordanting cotton; alum, chrome, iron, tin or copper can be used after the preceding processes. If souring has been left out the tannin can be added to the alum mordant.

Recipe

120 g (4 oz) cotton yarn
60 g (2 oz) alum
7 g (¼ oz) washing soda
7 g (¼ oz) tannic acid if the cotton has not been soured
4.5 litres (1 gallon) water

1 Dissolve the alum and washing soda in boiling water and add to the rest of the water.

2 Enter the wetted-out fibre.

3 Slowly bring to the boil and allow to boil for 1 hour.

4 Allow the water to cool and then add the tannic acid if the yarn has not been soured.

5 Simmer for 1 hour, stirring occasionally.

6 Leave the yarn in the bath over night.

7 Next morning, remove yarn, squeeze out the excess liquid and rinse.

8 It is now in a good state for dyeing, that is to say, evenly damp throughout.

The yarn can be dried and labelled for future use.

Effects of different mordants on cotton

Alum This mordant is most commonly used along with a small amount of washing soda. It should not affect the colour expected from the dyestuff.

Chrome Especially good when using brown dyes. If dyeing with cutch give the yarn an after-chrome bath.

Iron By adding iron the colour will be darkened. Steep the cotton in a cold solution of the mordant after dyeing.

Tin This will brighten the colours when used in conjunction with other mordants.

Copper sulphate Occasionally copper is added to the dyebath to vary the shades of brown or yellow. Copper is not a particularly common mordant amongst British dyers; it is possibly more popular in the United States.

Tannin (tannic acid)

Tannin helps the cotton to attract the dyestuff and to retain it. Tannic acid is free from any other colouring matter and is used for pale and bright shades. When dyeing darker shades, substances containing tannic acid can be used, such as sumach leaves or oak galls. Half a kilogram (1 lb) of tannic acid is the equivalent of 2 kg (4.5 lb) of sumach or 5 kg (11 lb) of oak galls.

Quantities of mordants

Use double the amounts given for wool and follow the general instructions for mordanting wool (page 36). Remember that cotton can stand boiling, alkaline liquor and sudden changes of temperature.

Dyeing

A few suggestions follow for using natural dyes on cotton. On the whole root and bark dyes are more satisfactory than petals, berries and stems.

Weld

Dye as for wool, using 180 g (6 oz) of weld for 120 g (4 oz) of cotton (page 50).

Resulting colours from each of the four mordants.

Alum — creamy yellow

Chrome — slightly warmer creamy yellow

Iron — buff

Tin — pale lemon yellow

Onion skins
Onion skins can be prepared and used as for wool (page 52).
Resulting colours:

Alum — ripe corn

Chrome — deep beige

Iron — drab

Tin — golden orange

Madder
Dye as for wool, remembering to use hard water. In order to build up a shade and to get good depth of colour repeat the dyeing processes several times.
Resulting colours from one dye-bath:

Alum — rose pink

Chrome — wild rose

Iron — dusky pink

Tin — clear pink

Cochineal
Cochineal can be used as for wool, but deeper shades would be obtained if the quantity of dyestuff were doubled.
Resulting colours:

Alum — sugary pink

Chrome — lilac pink

Iron — dull pink

Tin — clear pink

Indigo
Dye as for wool (page 56). The colours will not be as fast as those on wool, but if they fade they will fade attractively. By repeated dippings a dark blue will be obtained. Keep using the dye until the colour is exhausted — the shades will range from almost navy blue to a delicate sky blue. Extra samples will be useful for top-dyeing with yellow to make green and with red to make purple.

Walnut
Mercerized cotton becomes medium brown, while plain cotton tends to be a greyish-fawn when dyed without a mordant in green walnuts.

Lichen
Lichen which dyes brown on wool will give a light biscuit colour on plain cotton, while a lichen such as cudbear will give a pinky lilac colour.

Elderberries
Elderberries have little effect on cotton mordanted in alum, chrome or iron, but in tin a beautiful mauve is produced.

Blackberries
Ripe blackberries do not give a very strong colour on cotton mordanted in alum, chrome or iron, but a dramatic colour change affects cotton mordanted in tin. It changes to a strong, clear purple. Alum gives a dull pinky shade.

Cutch
See Historical Dyes, page 65.

Linen

Linen requires similar treatment to cotton. Scouring and bleaching need careful attention and the skeins, as always, must be thoroughly wetted out. Much linen is used in natural, half-bleached and bleached states. Most dye recipes given for cotton will work on linen; it may be advantageous to lengthen the boiling time, except in the case of madder.

Silk

There are two main classes of silk, wild silk and cultivated mulberry silk.

Tussah is the most important wild silk, and it is a brown colour. It is prepared and dyed in a similar way to cultivated silk. Cultivated silk is the product of the silkworm, the caterpillar of the *Bombyx mori* moth. It can be highly twisted or lightly twisted according to the requirements of the weaver. Spun silk is manufactured from partly reeled or damaged cocoons.

The silk fibre is surrounded by cream coloured or bright yellow gum, which could weigh 25 percent of the whole. It is soluble in dilute soap solution. This natural gum has to be removed before dyeing.

De-gumming recipe
40 g (1½ oz) soap to 4.5 litres (1 gallon) soft water

1 Make up a solution of the soap in 4.5 litres (1 gallon of soft water.

2 Submerge the skeins of silk in the bath by suspending them on a broad, smooth ribbon. Never let the silk float on its own in the dye-bath. This would result in much tangling.

3 Raise the temperature almost to the boil (90°C) for 1½ hours.

4 Allow to cool and then squeeze the skeins.

5 Repeat the process in a fresh solution.

6 Wash well in soapy water.

Points to note
Weak alkalis such as soap and ammonia scarcely affect silk. Hot caustic soda dissolves it completely.

Hydrogen of peroxide is in general use for bleaching purposes.

De-gumming should bring out silk's most valuable qualities i.e. its lustre and softness.

Boiled-off liquor can be added to the dye-bath to promote level dyeing (pages 40, 41).

Mordanting silk
Alum is the chief mordant used on silk but the others can be used with care. Chrome will enrich the colours, iron will darken and tin brighten. In the case of iron and tin it is advisable to use them very sparingly. Add a small quantity at the end of dyeing. Remove the silk first before stirring in the dissolved chemical.

Mordanting with alum
120 g (4 oz) clean de-gummed silk
30 g (1 oz) alum
4.5 litres (1 gallon) soft water

1 Dissolve alum and add it to bath.

2 Enter silk at 60°C and work for 30–45 minutes.

3 Remove from heat and let it steep for another 24 hours.

4 Rinse and dye.

Hints
1 Do not use loose dyestuff in the bath. Either strain the liquid or place the dyestuff in muslin or plastic netting.

2 Weigh twice the amount of dyestuff given in recipes for wool because silk does not have as great an affinity for dyestuffs as wool and it should be dyed at a lower temperature in order to preserve the lustre. Apart from that, dye as for wool.

3 It is often advisable to leave the silk steeping in the dye-bath overnight; this may increase fastness and depth of colour.

4 Thorough rinsing should follow.

5 Dry in the shade.

Weld was one of the dyestuffs which was particularly recommended for silk.

Recipes for silk
(Remember to double the quantity of dyestuff as given in wool recipes but use the same amount of mordant.)

Indigo
Use the recipe as for wool (page 57). Longer dips will probably be required to get a good depth of colour.

Crimson
Mordant with alum and dye with cochineal. Tin can be used sparingly to brighten the colour. Wash very thoroughly in soap after dyeing to avoid the tin making the yarn brittle.

Vermilion
Mordant with alum and dye with madder in hard water. Do not let it boil. A little soap and tin added towards the end of dyeing will brighten the colour.

Yellow
There are a number of dyes which could be used, including weld, flavine and fustic. For weld one

Samples dyed with woad

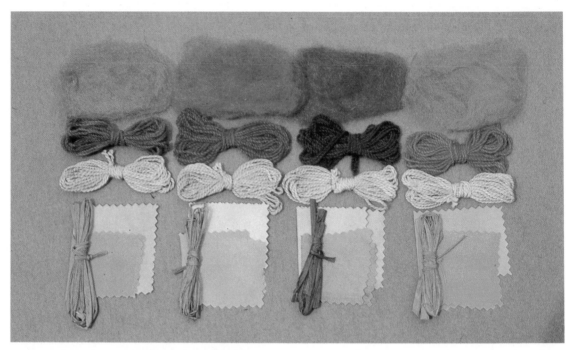

Onion skin dye used with four mordants. The dyed materials
are (from top): fleece, wool, cotton, raffia, silk and cotton cloth

Yarns dyed with stinging nettles, golden rod, weld and elder
leaves

and a half times the weight of silk will be required, so for 120 g (4 oz) of silk use 180 g (6 oz) weld. The result will be a beautiful clear lemon yellow with an alum mordant, a golden yellow from chrome mordant, dull olive from iron and a sharp bright yellow from tin.

As Bancroft pointed out, a much smaller quantity of quercitron is needed to obtain yellow — only 10–20 percent of the weight of yarn compared with 150 percent of weld. However, if weld grows wild in the garden or waste ground, it is worth harvesting one's own supply.

Charts of experiments with natural dyes

The following charts show the results of dyeing silk, linen, viscose rayon and nylon with natural dyes. The first chart shows the resulting colours when silk material was dyed with wool recipes and in the same dye-bath as the wool.

Dye	Alum	Chrome	Iron	Tin
Onion skins	Bright golden yellow	Deeper gold	Greenish-brown	Brassy yellow
Weld	Light lemon yellow	Warm yellow	Drab	Clear lemon yellow
Golden rod	Light yellow	Pale yellow	Deep fawn	Clear yellow
Elderberries	Light mauve	Slate grey	Dark grey	Clear mauve
Blackberries	Dull raspberry	Pale dull pink	Dull mauve	Brilliant violet
Cochineal	Crimson	Mauvish-pink	Deep purple	Scarlet
Madder	Light vermilion	Warm buff	Warm brownish-pink	Light brownish-pink

No mordants were used with walnuts and lichens.

Walnut: clear strong brown

Lichen: warm beige

Lichen (cudbear): purplish magenta
(raffia and sisal also dyed magenta in this bath).

Observations

Colours took well on silk material; they were much deeper than on cotton which was dyed in the same bath.

I was surprised by the brilliant violet produced by a tin mordant used with blackberries.

Mixed colours can be obtained in the usual way and silk can be top-dyed:

Orange

Mix madder and fustic.

Green

Any yellow dye plus indigo. Clear yellows give good greens while dull yellows make muddy greens.

Purple

Dye with indigo and then use cudbear, which does not need a mordant.

Black

Mordant with alum. Use logwood, with a small amount of flavine and 7 g (¼ oz) iron.

Brown

Mordant with 7 g (¼ oz) copper sulphate, then dye with madder and fustic chips.

It is always worth dyeing some silk at the same time as wool. The colour may be paler, but it could look very attractive when added to a piece of weaving.

The following chart shows the results from mordanting and dyeing linen threads.

Dye	Alum	Chrome	Iron	Tin
Golden rod	Pale lemon	Pale lemon	Dull cream	Clear yellow
Weld	Pale yellow	Pale yellow	Fawn	Clear pale yellow
Onion skins	Beige	Beige	Deep fawn	Golden yellow
Madder	Light pink	Warm pink	Mauvish-pink	Bright pink
Elderberry	Greyish-mauve on each sample			

Observations

Linen mordanted in tin showed the best colour.

Weld: iron and tin mordants affected the colour more than alum and chrome.

Onion skins: a good range from light gold to beige was obtained.

Madder: attractive shades of pink were obtained.

Elderberry: little difference was seen in the colours; they were all a greyish-mauve.

These experiments were carried out on continuous filament viscose rayon yarns (of the 'ribbonfil' standard and high tenacity types) manufactured by Courtaulds Limited of Coventry.

Dye		Alum	Chrome	Iron	Tin
Madder	T	Warm pinky-fawn	Light pink	Greyish-pink	Pinkish-cream
	V	Pinky-pale fawn	Pale pink	Dirty pink	Warm beige
Cochineal	T	Purplish-crimson	Pale mauve	Purplish-grey	Deep pink
	V	Deep mauve	Mauve	Greyish-mauve	Clear bright pink
Logwood	T	Bluish-purple	Very slightly deeper than alum	A deeper shade than chrome	Clear violet
	V	Light bluish-purple	Very similar to textured viscose	Violet	Lighter clear violet
Fustic chips	T	Clear yellow	Deeper yellow than alum	Dark dull yellow	Similar to alum
	V	Mustard yellow	Clear bright yellow	Dull yellow	Dull mustard yellow

T = textured viscose

V = high tenacity viscose yarn

Observations

Madder

Alum: Warm pink shades were developed, while in the same dye-bath wool turned vermilion.

Chrome: The colours lost their warm pink colouring and appeared dull

Iron: Had a greying effect on the colours.

Tin: Colours were a pinkish cream with a suggestion of orange. Bright orange was obtained from this dye-bath on wool.

There was slight fading on each sample after four weeks in a sunny window.

Fustic chips

The colours were not affected so much by the mordants. There was a little fading on each sample, but not as much as I would have expected with yellow.

Logwood chips
The tin mordant brought out violet shades, but the colours obtained from all mordants blended together well. Alum and chrome had similar effects. The colours faded after four weeks in a sunny window.

Cochineal
Each colour was very definitely affected by the different mordants; they included maroon, silvery pink, slatish-purple and deep sugary pink. The sample mordanted with tin showed more loss of colour than the others.

Samples of nylon yarn were mordanted as for wool and dyed in the same dye-bath with the wool. The following results were obtained.

Dye	Alum	Chrome	Iron	Tin	Light fastness
Golden rod	Lemon yellow	Bright lemon yellow	Dull lemon yellow	Clear greenish-yellow	No loss of colour apart from tin-mordanted yarn
Weld	Pale golden yellow	Rich golden yellow	Light khaki	Clear yellow	Very slight loss of colour
Onion skins	Deep gold	Brighter gold	Darker gold	Clear bright gold	Slight fading but not on chrome-mordanted yarn
Madder	Light vermilion	Vermilion	Brownish-tan	Bright orange	Slight fading on iron-mordanted yarn
Cochineal	Rusty red	Deep brick red	Rusty tan	Deep scarlet	Very slight fading. No loss of colour with tin mordant
Elderberry	Greyish-mauve	Grey	Mauve	Bluish-purple	Each sample faded

Observations

With golden rod, chrome gave the strongest colour.

Weld: the colours were strong and clear, not as lemon yellow as I would have expected, with the exception of tin-mordanted nylon.

Onion skins: the colours were more golden and brassy than those on wool.

Madder: iron made the most difference to the colour.

Cochineal: not as crimson and purple as I would have expected.

Elderberry: the colours were rather dull. Tin made the strongest colour.

9
Using Colour

Having made the colours and dyed the material we come to what some people find the most difficult part: these colours have to be used. Should we work instinctively or emotionally with our colours, or should we approach them through scientific theories? There was a time when colour theories were carefully studied, but they have now become unfashionable.

It is not necessary to study colour theories in great detail, although it is very interesting to do so, but it is useful to get into the habit of analysing colour schemes. Ancient textiles are often thrilling in their use and arrangement of colours. The creators of those materials probably worked from inspiration; they would not have depended on scientific colour theories. Young children work fearlessly with colour and can attain wonderful results. The woven tapestries by the children of Harrania in Egypt illustrate this. It does not follow that the more colours one has, the better the colour scheme. The Apocalypse tapestries in Angers use madder, walnut and indigo as the basis of the colour schemes.

Sources of inspiration

We need to train the eyes to analyse colour schemes. It is helpful to try to work out why certain colour arrangements are appealing.

Nature provides dozens of ideas. Looking at autumn leaves, birds' feathers, sea-shells, pebbles, rocks, wild birds' eggs, butterfly wings, precious stones, the sea, the sky, moorlands and landscapes will reveal wonderful colour schemes. Only it is not enough to look; it is necessary to analyse the proportion of one colour to another, to consider the depth and texture of the colour. We must examine the tone values, the brightness, the distribu-

tion. Equal quantities of two colours may look horrible but the slightest touch of one might be just what was wanted. Look at the colours in pansies, in violets, or consider the delicate pink of a wild rose with just a few dark brown stamens. Find a lovely colour scheme in nature and then use it as a starting point.

There are other sources of inspiration: perhaps a stained glass window, a painting or an ancient textile. Choice of colour is such a personal matter. In my teaching experience I have met just a few pupils and students who had a wonderful colour sense and who could use colours in a way I envied.

One of the simplest ways to start is to consider the three primary colours. To an artist mixing paints, these are red, yellow and blue. To a scientist working with coloured lights they are red, yellow and green. Blue and yellow paints or dyes will make green, but blue and yellow light will make white.

Making a colour circle with fleece

Take the three primary colours provided by cochineal, onion skins and indigo. Arrange these in a circle and then blend each colour so that they gradually merge into each other.

Inside the circle arrange another ring of colours by blending each colour with white. Outside the circle repeat this process but use black fleece.

Another way of training the eye to analyse colour is to collect samples of coloured threads and arrange them in a spectrum. Or see how many colours can be collected from colour magazines; cut them into squares and make a mosaic. Colours chosen might be cold, hot, bright or dull. Patterns may emerge which could be used in patchwork.

The colour circle can help in the choice of com-

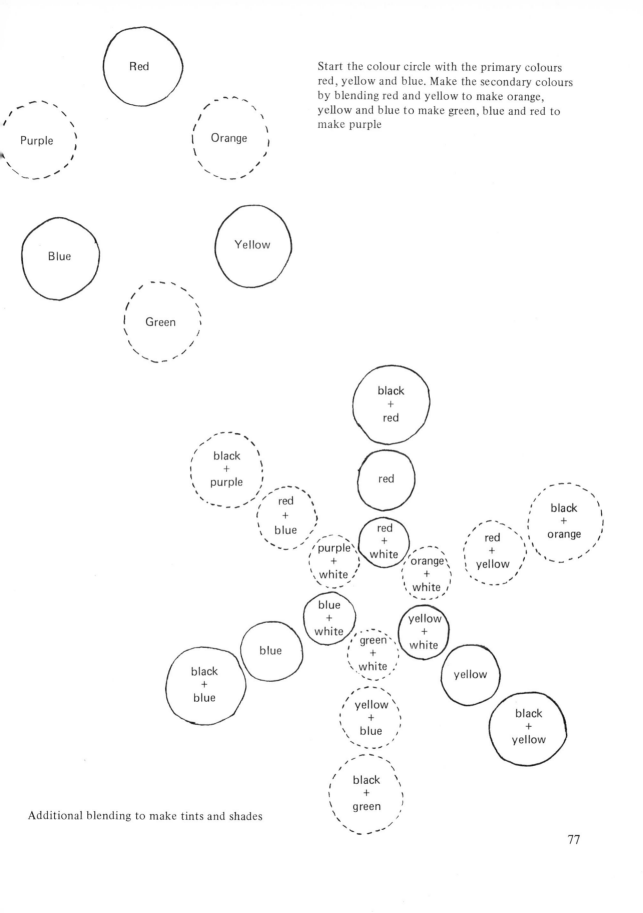

Red

Purple

Orange

Start the colour circle with the primary colours red, yellow and blue. Make the secondary colours by blending red and yellow to make orange, yellow and blue to make green, blue and red to make purple

Blue

Yellow

Green

black
+
red

black
+
purple

red

red
+
blue

purple
+
white

red
+
white

orange
+
white

red
+
yellow

black
+
orange

blue
+
white

yellow
+
white

black
+
blue

blue

green
+
white

yellow

black
+
yellow

yellow
+
blue

black
+
green

Additional blending to make tints and shades

77

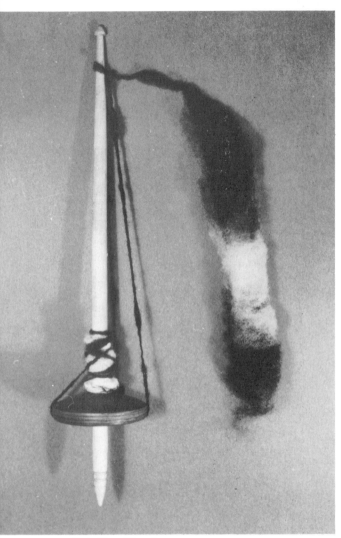

Spindle with rolag

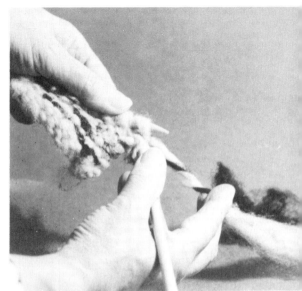

Knitting with fleece

Blending fleece

Fleece can be blended carefully in order to obscure individual colours and make another, or it can be lightly mixed in order to allow one colour to float over another. Short lengths can be designed by blending fleece in the fingers and finger-spinning a yarn and then plying it by letting it twist back on itself. Such yarns are very useful for collage work in embroidery, adding colour and texture to weaving and for knitting. Carders are used to brush the colours and make well-mixed blends.

Impressionist painters show how effective it is to use pure colours in spots and leave our brains to do the mixing. Bernat Klein in his book *Eye for Colour* describes how his designs were influenced by looking at a Seurat painting. When he started painting he saw everything in terms of colour and cloth. He said colour was all around him, 'pursuing and cajoling' him.

When blending fleece, intermediate grades from the palest tint to the darkest tone of the colour can be obtained by varying the proportions of white or black in relation to the colour.

Plan of grey mixtures
Work on a basis of ten parts.

| White | 10 | 9 | 8 | 7 | 6 | 5 | 4 | 3 | 2 | 1 | – |
| Black | – | 1 | 2 | 3 | 4 | 5 | 6 | 7 | 8 | 9 | 10 |

plementary colours or discords. Those colours which are opposite each other in the circle are complementaries. Often a small amount of one with a large amount of the other will look attractive, while equal quantities could cancel each other out. Discords need careful handling; they are made by using a dark tone of a light colour with a light tone of a dark colour e.g. yellow ochre with mauve.

Colours can be made lighter or darker by blending fleece before spinning, by plying different colours together after spinning or by mixing colours in the warp and weft of a piece of weaving.

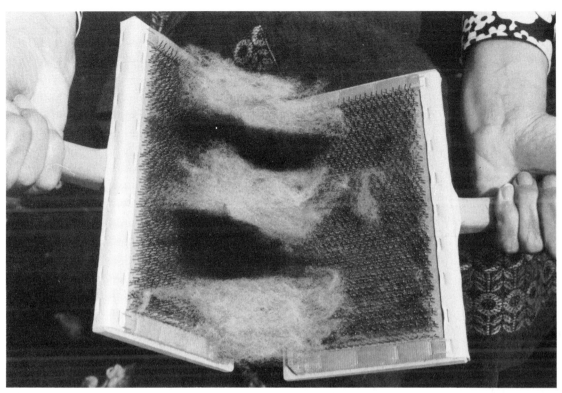

Carding two colours   *Below* Rolling a striped rolag

Knitted waistcoat from blended wool

By starting with ten parts white and diminishing that number by one each time, you will reach black at the other end of the scale.

When colour blending it is essential to consider the quality of the wool (page 19).

Effect of black and white

Black helps to produce rich, dark coloured threads, while white, with its great reflecting power, has a subduing influence on the colour elements. It always appears more prominent than the colour with which it is combined. Because of this, colours are examined, compared and matched to the best advantage when placed on a dull black ground.

The plan given for grey mixtures can be used for other colour mixtures; each colour can be blended with white, with black or with grey. Having explored the possibilities of one colour, blend red through orange to yellow, yellow through green to blue, and blue through violet to red. Each blend can then be made darker or lighter by being blended with black, natural or white.

When designing the colour blends, consider the end product. If the yarn is to be made into a tweed coat it would probably look odd if lumps of one colour appeared in a haphazard or random way; on the other hand if the colours floated in a rhythmical regular pattern the material could glow most attractively.

80

Carding

When blending fleece on the carders it can be arranged in blocks so that the spun threads appear to have been tie-dyed. It is necessary to place an odd number of stripes on the carders so that the colours correspond when being transferred one to the other. See diagrams on page 82.

Spinning

Threads can be tightly or loosely spun or they can be made into fancy spun threads. Little coloured beads of fibre, called knops, which have been rolled and felted, can be added during carding. This will produce a yarn with rough characteristics. Knops could be the same colour as those used in the background, e.g. blue and white on a pale blue ground, or they may contrast, several coloured knops being added to give a jewel-like appearance.

Knitted coat from blended wool spun and knitted by Heather Tredgett

Plying

If fibres have been dyed in spun form, colour mixing can be carried out by twisting two or more threads together, e.g. black and colour, white and colour, grey and colour, colour and colour.

When mixing tone and tone, hue and hue or tone and hue, the skill of the individual will be very evident. Different thicknesses of threads can be plied together, or a variety of fibres and textures can be used. Spinners will see possibilities with slub yarns, gimp, bouclé, and Z and S twists.

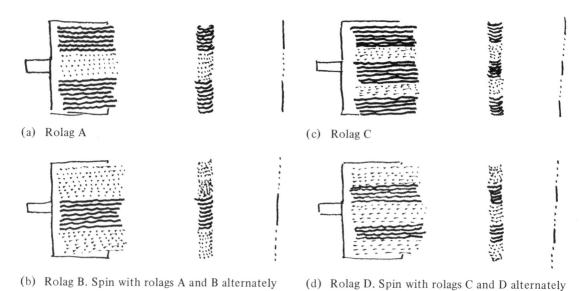

(a) Rolag A

(c) Rolag C

(b) Rolag B. Spin with rolags A and B alternately

(d) Rolag D. Spin with rolags C and D alternately

Colour and weave

Weavers can discover unusual and attractive colour mixtures by using their dyed threads in a small sampler.

Make a warp consisting of six stripes in two colours, each one about 5cm (2in.) wide. The first and last stripes should be solid colour.

Cross the warp in the same colour arrangement. Weave 30 cm (12 in.) in tabby, followed by two and two twill, three and one twill and hopsack. This will give a sampler 120 cm (48 in.) long with 144 small squares to consider. Make the warp long enough for other colours to be used in the weft. Colour changes in stripes can be emphasized by denting.

Colour A		1A	1B		2A	2B		3A	1B		4A	4B		Colour B

5 cm (2 in.)

Other suggestions for using dyed fleece and yarn

Fleece and individually designed yarn will be a great source of inspiration to those who embroider. Backgrounds can be decorated by the addition of special threads or by finger-twisted fleece.

When designing clothes or furnishings there should be no problem over matching colours, if the whole project is planned from the beginning. However, beginners are more likely to find themselves with a large number of small skeins and samples. These can be used for patchwork, the pieces being woven, knitted or crocheted. If rags have also been dyed, they will make colourful rag rugs. John Hinchcliffe's book *Rugs from Rags* is specially recommended as a valuable guide.

Small quantities of threads can also be used to make decorative hangings on twigs, wire, coathangers, picture frames or polystyrene dishes.

Tie-dyeing

Skeins, or warps or cloth can be tie-dyed to make a wide variety of patterns. Many beautiful examples of this work can be seen in museums. The threads or cloth are tied tightly in order to stop the dye

By using two dyes, yellow and red, the skein
will have lengths of white, orange, yellow and red

(a) White skein

(b) Skein tied at both ends

(c) Bind the skein tightly at A and B. Place skein
in yellow dye

(d) Untie binding at B

(e) Bind the skein at C, thus protecting yellow
strip. Place skein in red dye. Untie binding
at A and C

Yellow + Red   White   Yellow   Red   Yellow + Red
Orange   Orange   Orange
Yellow

(f)

Orange   Orange   Red   Orange
White
Orange   White   Yellow   Red   Orange
Orange

(g)

A green warp with blue and white stripes. Dye the
warp yellow. Untie the binding with one knot

(at A). Dye the warp blue. Untie the binding
with two knots (at B)

from penetrating the material. It can be done at
random or to a pre-arranged pattern.

The warp can be made in a white, light or natural
colour. Make sure that the end loops and the cross
are tied very securely before dyeing, for loose
threads could be disastrous. Ikat is the name used
to describe a tie-dyed warp: double-ikat describes
cloth which has a tie-dyed warp and weft. The Jap-
anese term for this is *kasuri*. Warp threads are
usually packed closely into the reed so that the
weft does not hide the pattern. Alternatively, if
the warp is widely spaced as in rug weaving, a weft-
faced material can be made from tie-dyed skeins.

Warps could be made in narrow strips to make
them easy to handle.

Fast colours

The question of fast colours and fading is bound
to be a problem to all dyers. Some colours fade
more than others. This will depend on the dyestuff, the fibre and the use to which the material
is put. Curtains at a sunny window face a severe
test.

Many ways of testing colours can be devised.
It is a good idea to keep an accurate record through-

Crochet squares from dyed samples of yarn

out the dyeing process and finish by carrying out a thorough fading test.

Fleece, threads or material can be placed in a sunny window or in a greenhouse and left for a measured length of time. There are machines for testing colours; these light simulators can give the equivalent of a certain number of days of sunshine in a few hours.

It is always a consolation to me when I remember a lecture on 'Colour in Scottish Textiles'. The speaker said 'No dyed shade is absolutely fast, for fastness is only relative, but good dyed shades are fast compared with most *natural* shades'. Natural colours of wools and hairs are hardly ever fast. Think of the faded locks on a dark sheep, or the golden light on the ends of the children's hair at the seaside. A story is told of one of the old Scots dyers put 'on the mat' for a complaint of fading of slate grey. He replied: 'If the Loard canna dye a cuddy a guid fast shade, hoo dae ye expect me tae manage it?'

Colours are affected by sun, air, water, and by rubbing. The faded look can be very fashionable — think of the popularity of faded blue jeans. Natural dyes, when they fade, usually fade in an even, mellow way. The least pleasant examples of fading are those of the foliage on seventeenth and eighteenth-century tapestries, which has faded from green to blue. But one cannot say that for the beautiful restricted colour range to be seen on the Lady and Unicorn tapestries in the Cluny Museum, Paris, or the Hunting tapestries in the Victoria and Albert Museum, London.

The main secret of getting good fast colours is to mordant thoroughly and to choose dyestuff and fibre carefully.

Testing dyes

Keep some of each sample tested in a dark place so that it can be used as a control sample. These are simple tests which will act as a rough guide to the fastness of the threads.

Light fastness

Expose yarn to sunlight for a few weeks. During this time compare sample with the control at intervals. Look for any fading or change. Mounted samples could show different lengths of time. It would only be a rough guide because amounts of sunshine vary.

Testing yarns for fading

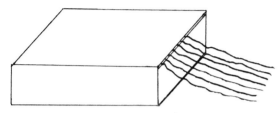

Half the yarn is shut in the box while the other half is exposed to sunlight

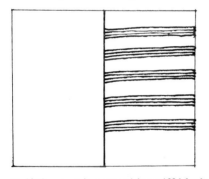

Half the yarn is covered by stiff black card

Washing fastness

1 Attach threads to a white cloth of similar material or plait them with undyed threads. Bring to the boil in a saucepan of soapy water and then simmer for 15 minutes.

2 Proceed as for experiment 1 but use three types of detergents, mild, strong and biological.

Check for bleeding of the dye into the soapy water, loose colour on the white material and the shade compared with original sample.

Dry rubbing test

Rub the fibres with a piece of dry white cloth. Check to see if any colour has rubbed off and marked the cloth.

Wet rubbing test

Use wet fibres. Press them dry between white cloth and look for loose colour.

These tests will give a rough idea of the quality and reliability of the dyes. Look to see if the colour is lighter, darker or patchy. Feel the fibre to see if it has become harder, felted, or whether it has shrunk.

Molly Duncan in her book *Spin your own Wool, and Dye it and Weave it* reports on tests which were made on New Zealand dyeing. (Many of the colours I saw in New Zealand, which were obtained from natural dyes, were extremely clear and bright). As a result of their tests on a laboratory 'dye-fading' machine, bright yellow shades were the first to change.

Pigeon berries (porokaiwhiri) mordanted with alum and cream of tartar gave a soft canary-yellow which faded within one day in bright sunlight. The same berries mordanted with chrome gave a ginger gold shade which was satisfactory in the fading machine.

Puriri berries mordanted with alum and cream of tartar gave a rich purplish-brown which was a fast colour.

The seed-pods of New Zealand flax (*phormium tenax*) gave excellent results for fastness. Shades of tan were produced according to the strength of the dye-bath.

All colours from lichen, with the exception of the bright yellows, were satisfactory.

Parsley mordanted with copper sulphate produced a fast green.

Other light tests

I tested a range of colours which had been dyed on a variety of threads. They were hung in a sunny window and exposed to the sun for one, two and four weeks. One section was always kept covered. The samples which showed greatest loss of colour were those dyed with cudbear. After four weeks some of the rayon and cotton samples were fading slightly.

The Colour Museum, Bradford, Yorkshire

There is a very interesting Colour Museum in Bradford which would be well worth a visit for those people who wish to learn more about colour. It was opened in 1978 and is organized by the Society of Dyers and Colourists. This Society was formed in Bradford in 1884 and its interests include every aspect of colour and coloration. The Society's Royal Charter, granted in 1963, requires it to promote the advancement of the science of colour and to stimulate education in the interests of coloration 'in all aspects of human life'.

Exhibitions are arranged in the Museum, including 'The World of Colour' and 'The Science of Colour'. A section deals with the natural colouring matters used by industrial dyers and artists' colourmen before the Chemical Revolution of the mid-nineteenth century. 'The Creation of an Industry' tells the story of W.H. Perkin and the manufacture of the first synthetic dye.

By making prior arrangements one is allowed to study from a large collection of reference books and to look at old books of dyed samples. These books contain samples and recipes showing a variety of subtle shades which were obtained by careful mixing of such dyes as fustic, madder, logwood, cochineal, indigo and other woods.

Admission to the Museum is free. It is open to the public on Tuesday to Friday 2 p.m. – 5 p.m. and on Saturday 10 a.m. – 4 p.m. It is closed on Sundays, Mondays and Public Holidays.

The address is: The Colour Museum, The Society of Dyers and Colourists, Perkin House, P.O. Box 244, 82 Grattan Road, Bradford, West Yorkshire, BD1 2JB.

In 1971 the Colour Education Committee of the Society was established in order to provide additional training in the basic facts of colour for teachers.

10
Dyeing Worldwide

Every part of the world will produce something which can be used in natural dyeing, and an interest in this subject has led many people to travel widely in search of colours and special recipes. Often the same dyestuffs are used in different countries, but the colours may be different because of local conditions.

America

Brooklyn Botanical Garden, New York
The Brooklyn Botanical Garden is in the heart of the city of New York. Since 1910 it has been 'committed to the refreshment, enjoyment and instruction of its visitors'. Twelve thousand different

Dyeing at the Brooklyn Botanic Garden, USA

kinds of plants grow on the 50 acres. The garden is open free to the public 365 days a year. In 1964 the Garden started giving classes on the use of plants in dyeing to adult students, and recently there have also been children's classes. 'Show and tell' lectures are arranged on the subject of Dye Plants and Dyeing, and samples of dyed yarns are kept for these lectures. Valuable handbooks are published. Two which are of great intereat to dyers are *Natural Plant Dyeing* Vol. 29 No. 2 and *Dye Plants and Dyeing* Vol. 20 No. 3

Elizabeth Scholtz, the Vice-President of the Brooklyn Botanical Garden, has travelled round the world gathering information on dye-plants and how to use them. The handbooks contain practical hints and useful articles which have been contributed by dyers all round the world.

The Handweavers' Guild of America.

This Guild was started in the summer of 1969 by a handful of spinners, weavers and dyers. Their magazine, *Shuttle, Spindle and Dyepot*, first published in December 1969, has grown from 18 pages to almost 100 today, with colour. The number of Guilds throughout the United States is continually growing. Some have over 300 members, some as few as ten. Larger Guilds send out monthly newsletters listing meetings, exhibitions and demonstrations.

The Guild in Wisconsin has established a dyers' garden in co-operation with the Boener Botanical Gardens, Whitnall Park, Milwaukee. This garden provides the public with information on natural dye sources and encourages the introduction of dye plants in private gardens. Guild members arrange demonstrations of natural dyeing. It is interesting to note that there is no ban on growing woad in Wisconsin, but the State Department of Agriculture suggested that it should be grown with caution in order to eliminate any danger of weed infestation.

Australia

Guilds of spinners, dyers and weavers in Australia have made a number of experiments with natural dyes, particularly with leaves from various species of eucalyptus. Mrs J. Carman, who lives in Melbourne, Victoria, collected leaves from over 130 species of eucalyptus. She used alum, copper sulphate, iron and tin as mordants. The usual method of cutting up leaves and boiling them in soft water was followed. Leaves which were dried before dyeing gave more consistent colours. Good colours were obtained on Border Leicester wool, while Merino wool gave softer shades. The colours did not fade after careful washing and they were not greatly affected by light. With alum mordant red, orange, yellow and olive green colours were obtained. Copper sulphate produced shades of green and brown; tin gave yellow shades and iron produced varying shades of grey. The strongest red dye was obtained from *Eucalyptus cordata*, which is native to Tasmania. The most intense colours were obtained during a hot dry summer. More details are given in *Natural Plant Dyeing* Vol. 29 No. 2.

Darrel Bailey is another Australian dyer, who lives in Sydney. He is a keen natural dyer and from his interest has grown a business which has worldwide connections. His favourite dyes are indigo, three types of cochineal, madder, fustic, logwood, cutch, walnut, red sandalwood and archil from the Great Barrier Reef. These give him a reliable range of good, fast colours. Most of his dyes are grown in Queensland where there is a wide climatic range. His dyes have been accepted in the major museums and institutions including the Smithsonian Institute. They are also used by restorers of Persian rugs. He cannot grow weld as it is classed as a noxious weed, so he uses fustic.

New Zealand

Some of the clearest and strongest colours dyed with plants are to be found in New Zealand. Joyce Lloyd and Molly Duncan have achieved very interesting results when using different parts of the New Zealand flax plant *Phormium tenax*. Dyes are obtained from the flowers, stalks, seed-pods, leaves and roots.

This is a list of their results, as given in *Natural Plant Dyeing* Vol. 29 No. 2.

Flowers and buds:
Alum – pinky fawn shades and tans
Iron and copper – shades of brown
Aluminium and soda – pinky fawn
Cream of tartar and tin – apricot shades

Leaves:

Alum plus iodized salt — pink

Base of leaf with alum mordant — tan and apricot

Roots:

Alum — light brown

Alum and soda — chocolate brown

Bichromate of potash — good fawn shades

Cream of tartar and tin — light golden brown

Flower stalks:

Alum — fawn shades

Equal quantities of dyestuff and wool were used.

Phormium tenax produces fibres used by the Maoris for their *piu piu* (flax skirts). The bark of the Raurekau produces red dye and black is obtained from *paru*, a special mud found only in certain areas of swamp lands. The sword-like leaves are scraped in pre-arranged places so that the fibres can absorb the dye and form a pattern on the skirt.

Guilds of Spinners, Dyers and Weavers

Guilds of Spinners, Dyers and Weavers are made up of enthusiastic and friendly people who are ready to share their knowledge and experience with others. Guilds flourish in the United States of America, Canada, Australia, New Zealand and South Africa.

In Great Britain the number of Guilds has increased rapidly. It is possible to attend meetings, demonstrations and workshops in most parts of the country. Every two years a summer school is organized by the Association of Guilds and it is held in different parts of the United Kingdom. Spinners, dyers and weavers from other countries are especially welcome. As well as this summer school, demonstrations and workshops are often held at week-ends in adult residential colleges. Suppliers of dyestuffs hold courses as do a number of craftsmen and women. Information about these courses is usually given in magazines, including *Crafts* which is published bi-monthly by the Crafts Council.

A few years ago members of Guilds in different parts of Britain arranged a project which involved dyeing with the same species of plant and then comparing the results to see how the habitat, environment, weather conditions and atmosphere affected the colours.

Using natural dyestuffs can become an absorbing hobby and can lead to all kinds of adventures when searching for an elusive colour or recipe.

Barbara Mullins, a well-known English weaver and dyer, has made a most interesting study of natural dyeing in Peru. She has brought back to England a large number of beautiful colours which she dyed while there.

Conclusion

On the whole it is not advisable to try to dye huge quantities of yarn with natural dyes, but small amounts of subtle colours can be introduced into one's work to add a very special effect. Sometimes natural dyed yarns are described as being dull and muddy: they do not need to be dull; with the right treatment the colours can be bright and glowing if that is what is required. By careful selection of mordants and dyestuffs colours can be produced to suit everyone's taste. Dyeing makes a fascinating and tantalizing hobby.

Glossary

Acetic acid Weak acid found in vinegar. It is used to neutralize alkaline water, develop colour from berry dyes and help set colours after dyeing.

Adjective dyes Dyes which require a mordant to fix the dye permanently to the fibre.

Alizarin Chemical name of the important colouring matter found in the madder root. In 1868 it was made from anthracene, derived from coal tar.

Alum Aluminium potassium sulphate, one of the most popular mordants.

Ammonia A chemical used for general purposes of neutralizing.

Argol The tartar deposited from wines completely fermented. Becomes cream of tartar when purified. It adds fullness and brilliancy to colour when used in conjunction with mordants.

Blending Mixing coloured fleece or different fibres before spinning.

Blooming Brightening colours by using tin. It is usually done before the end of dyeing and is followed by a soap bath.

Chrome Bichromate of potash, potassium dichromate or potassium bichromate. This is a very pleasant mordant to use. It is sensitive to light.

Cream of tartar See Argol.

De-gumming Removing gum, sericin, from silk, making it lustrous and soft.

Detergent A cleansing agent. Can be mild, strong or biological.

Dip Usually applied to immersing yarn or cloth in the blue vat during indigo dyeing.

Dye Colouring matter in solution.

Dye-bath Dye liquor diluted with water, also name given to a vessel which is used for dyeing.

Dye liquor Concentrated natural dye, also called 'ooze' in the USA.

Dye source The plant, animal or mineral source capable of producing a natural dye.

Dyestuff The material to be used in making a dye.

Enter To immerse the yarn in the mordant bath or dye.

Exhaust To use all the colour from a dye-bath.

Felt Matting of wool, caused by sudden temperature change, fast boiling or over-agitation. These processes can be carried out on purpose to produce felt.

Fugitive Dye that fades.

Glauber's salt Sodium sulphate.

Greening Bringing out green tones of a yellow dye by adding copper sulphate during dyeing.

Gummed (silk) Silk which is stiff and dull in appearance because it is coated with natural gum (sericin).

In the grease unwashed wool which still contains lanolin.

Iron Ferrous sulphate (copperas), green vitriol, a mordant used to darken colours (sadden).

Kemp A fibre with a well-developed medulla and no cortical layer. It resists dye.

Mercerized cotton Cotton prepared by treating with a concentrated solution of caustic soda. Discovered by John Mercer in 1844. Lustre and dyeing capacity are increased.

Mordant Mineral salt which fixes dye and makes the colour permanent.

Murray The colour of a mulberry, purple red.

Natural dye A dye obtained from a plant, animal or mineral source.

Pigment Insoluble colour, must be used in conjunction with some form of binding material for application to a surface.

Polygenetic colouring matters Dyestuffs which give different shades according to the mordant used.

Roving Fine continuous length of fibres prepared for spinning.

Saddening Making colours darker by mordanting with iron or copper sulphate after dyeing.

Scour To wash thoroughly and remove all impurities from wool.

Sectional dyeing Dyeing a section only of a skein.

Simmer To keep just below boiling point; could be a low simmer or a high simmer ($82^{\circ}C - 93^{\circ}C$).

Skein A hank of yarn.

Sliver Continuous length of fibre without twist.

Sodium carbonate Soda.

Sodium chloride Salt.

Sodium dithionite Formerly known as sodium hydrosulphite. Used when dyeing indigo and woad.

Sodium hydroxide Caustic soda, used with sodium dithionite when dyeing indigo and woad.

Spun silk Silk manufactured from damaged and partly reeled cocoons.

Staple The length of cotton or wool fibres.

Substantive dyes Dyes which colour yarn permanently without a mordant.

Suint Perspiration deposited on the surface of the fibre from the sweat gland which is near the root of the fibre.

Swift A skein holder.

Tie-dyeing Tightly binding threads, warp, cloth or garments so that some parts resist the dye.

Top A continuous roving consisting of combed fibres which have been prepared for spinning worsted threads.

Top-dyeing Dyeing one colour over another.

Vat A large tub or vessel. Also used to describe dyes which are not soluble in water.

Vinegar Diluted acetic acid.

Wetting-out Making the yarn wet right through to the centre.

Working the wool Turning, exposing or moving the wool gently with a rod while it is in the mordant or dye-bath to ensure even penetration.

Useful Addresses

Suppliers often change and lists can never be up to date. The safest way to find out the address of your nearest supplier is to refer to a journal, get in touch with a craft group or refer to the Public Library.

Chemists will supply a number of the ingredients required for dyeing, and supermarkets or household stores will supply common chemicals such as vinegar, salt and soda.

Great Britain

The Secretary,
Association of Guilds of Weavers, Spinners and
    Dyers,
London WC1N 3XX

Publish a quarterly journal

America

Handweavers' Guild of America, Inc.,
998 Farmington Avenue,
West Hartford,
Conn. 06107.
USA

Prepares the magazine Shuttle, Spindle and Dyepot, *and other publications, including a suppliers' directory of materials and equipment for dyers, spinners, and weavers ($2.00).*

New Zealand

Handweavers' Guild Inc.,
P.O. Box 24090,
Auckland
New Zealand

South Africa

Handweavers' Guild,
c/o St Paul's Road,
Houghton 2196
Johannesburg
South Africa

Bibliography

ARY, S. and GREGORY, M., *The Oxford Book of Wild Flowers*, Oxford University Press 1960.

BANCROFT, E., *The Philosophy of Permanent Colours*, 1794.

BOLTON, E., *Lichens for Vegetable Dyeing*, London Studio Books, 1960.

BRUNELLO, F., *The Art of Dyeing in the History of Mankind*, Neri Pozza Vicenza, 1973.

CHADWICK, E., *The Craft of Handspinning*, Batsford, 1980.

DAVENPORT, E.G., *Your Yarn Dyeing*, Sylvan Press, London, 1955.

DUNCAN, M., *Creative Crafts with Wool and Flax*, A.H. & A.W. Reed, Wellington, N.Z., 1971.

DUNCAN, M., *Spin Your Own Wool and Dye it and Weave it*, A.H. & A.W. Reed, Wellington, N.Z., 1968.

HALE, M.E., *Lichen Handbook: A Guide to the Lichens of Eastern North America*, Smithsonian Institute, Washington D.C., 1961.

HINCHCLIFFE, J. and JEFFS, A., *Rugs from Rags*, Orbis Publishing, London, 1977.

HORSFALL and LAWRIE, *The Dyeing of Textile Fibres*, Chapman & Hall, London, 1949.

HUMMEL, J.J., *The Dyeing of Textile Fabrics*, Cassell & Co., 1896.

HURRY, J.B., *The Woad Plant*, Oxford University Press, 1930.

KERSHAW, K.A. and ALVIN, K.L., *The Observer's Book of Lichens*, Frederick Warne & Co, London and New York, 1977.

KLEIN, B., *Eye for Colour*, Klein with Collins, London, 1965.

LEGGETT, W.F., *Ancient and Medieval Dyes*, Chemical Publishing Co. Inc., Brooklyn, N. York, 1944.

LLOYD, J., *Dyes from Plants of Australia and New Zealand*, Reed, 1968.

MABEY, R. *Plants with a Purpose*, Collins, 1977.

MAILE, A., *Tie-and-Dye as a Present Day Craft*, Mills & Boon, London, 1963.

MAIRET, E., *Vegetable Dyes*, Faber & Faber, London, 1944.

RAINEY, S., *Weaving Without a Loom*, Davis, Worcester, Mass., 1968.

RIPPENGAL, J., *How to Dye in Your Kitchen*, published privately by the author.

ROBERTSON, S., *Dyes from Plants*, Studio Vista, London & Van Nostrand Reinhold, New York, 1973.

ROBINSON, S., *A History of Dyed Textiles*, London, 1969.

THE SOCIETY OF DYERS AND COLOURISTS AND CONTRIBUTORS, *Introducing Colour*, The Society of Dyers and Colourists, 1975.

SCHULTZ, K., *Create your own Natural Dyes*, Sterling Publishing, New York, 1975.

THURSTAN, V., *The Use of Vegetable Dyes*, Dryad Press, Leicester, 1968.

WILLS, N.T., *Woad in the Fens*, Published privately by the Author, 1979.

HANDBOOKS (Special printing of *Plants and Gardens*)
Dye Plants and Dyeing, vol. 20 No. 3
Natural Plant Dyeing, vol. 29 No. 2
Published by Brooklyn Botanic Garden, New York.

Index